Teaching With Movies

★ ★ ★ ★ ★

Recreation, Sports, Tourism, and Physical Education

Teresa O'Bannon

Marni Goldenberg

Human Kinetics

Library of Congress Cataloging-in-Publication Data

O'Bannon, Teresa, 1969-
  Teaching with movies : recreation, sports, tourism, and physical education / Teresa O'Bannon, Marni Goldenberg.
    p. cm.
  Includes bibliographical references.
  ISBN-13: 978-0-7360-6508-5 (soft cover)
  ISBN-10: 0-7360-6508-3 (soft cover)
  1. Motion pictures in education--Catalogs. 2. Physical education and training. I. Goldenberg, Marni, 1972- II. Title.
  LB1044.Z9O32 2007
  371.33'523--dc22

                    2007013658

ISBN-10: 0-7360-6508-3
ISBN-13: 978-0-7360-6508-5

Copyright © 2008 by Teresa O'Bannon and Marni Goldenberg

The Web addresses cited in this text were current as of June 2007, unless otherwise noted.

Acquisitions Editor: Gayle Kassing, PhD; **Developmental Editor:** Ray Vallese; **Assistant Editor:** Derek Campbell; **Copyeditor:** Patsy Fortney; **Proofreader:** Darlene Rake; **Permission Manager:** Carly Breeding; **Graphic Designer:** Fred Starbird; **Graphic Artist:** Denise Lowry; **Cover Designer:** Keith Blomberg; **Photographer (cover):** Keith Blomberg; **Printer:** Versa Press

Printed in the United States of America   10 9 8 7 6 5 4 3 2 1

Human Kinetics
Web site: www.HumanKinetics.com

United States: Human Kinetics, P.O. Box 5076, Champaign, IL 61825-5076
800-747-4457
e-mail: humank@hkusa.com

Canada: Human Kinetics, 475 Devonshire Road Unit 100, Windsor, ON N8Y 2L5
800-465-7301 (in Canada only)
e-mail: orders@hkcanada.com

Europe: Human Kinetics, 107 Bradford Road, Stanningley, Leeds LS28 6AT, United Kingdom
+44 (0) 113 255 5665
e-mail: hk@hkeurope.com

Australia: Human Kinetics, 57A Price Avenue, Lower Mitcham, South Australia 5062
08 8372 0999
e-mail: info@hkaustralia.com

New Zealand: Human Kinetics, Division of Sports Distributors NZ Ltd.
P.O. Box 300 226 Albany, North Shore City, Auckland
0064 9 448 1207
e-mail: info@humankinetics.co.nz

Contents

Movie Finder

Title	Page	Rating	Scene selection	Activity	Coaching	Commercial recreation	Competition	Diversity	Environmental issues
13 Going on 30	1	PG-13	All/2	★					
50 First Dates	2	PG-13	All/2						
About Schmidt	4	R	All/2						
Ali	6	R	All/1				★		
Awakenings	8	PG-13	All/3						
Bad News Bears, The	10	PG	All/2		★		★		
Beach, The	12	R	All/3+						★
Bend It Like Beckham	14	PG-13	All/2		★			★	
Big	16	PG	All/2						
Billy Elliot	17	R	All	★				★	
Bobby Jones: Stroke of Genius	19	PG	All/3	★			★		
Born Into Brothels: Calcutta's Red Light Kids	21	R	All/3+					★	
Breaking Away	23	PG	All/2				★		
Cars	25	G	3						
Coach Carter	27	PG-13	All/2		★		★		
Cocoon	29	PG-13	All/3+						
Cutting Edge, The	31	PG	All/1		★		★		
Day After Tomorrow, The	33	PG-13	All/3+						★
Dirty Dancing	34	PG-13	2	★				★	
Dream Team, The	36	PG-13	1						
Eight Below	38	PG	All/2						

Family issues	Health and wellness	History	Inclusion	Leadership	Leisure behavior	Life stages	Outdoor recreation	Physical and mental challenge	Recreation therapy	Sport	Teamwork	Tourism and travel
					★	★						
	★		★						★			
★					★	★						★
		★								★		
					★				★			
★										★	★	
					★							★
★										★		
					★	★						
★					★							
★										★		
★					★							
										★	★	
												★
										★	★	
	★				★	★						
										★	★	
								★				
★												
									★		★	
				★			★	★				

(continued)

Title	Page	Rating	Scene selection	Activity	Coaching	Commercial recreation	Competition	Diversity	Environmental issues
Endurance, The: Shackleton's Legendary Antarctic Expedition	40	G	All						
Failure to Launch	42	PG-13	3+	★					
Fever Pitch	44	PG-13	3+						
For Love of the Game	46	PG-13	1	★					
Four Minutes	47	NR	All/1	★			★		
Friday Night Lights	49	PG-13	All/2		★			★	
Gentleman's Game, A	50	R	All/1	★	★				
Gladiator	52	R	All/2						
Glory Road	54	PG	All/3+		★		★	★	
Gods Must Be Crazy, The	56	PG	All/3+					★	
Greatest Game Ever Played, The	58	PG	All/1		★			★	
Hook	59	PG	All/3+						
Hoot	61	PG	2						★
Hotel Rwanda	63	PG-13	All						
Hudsucker Proxy, The	65	PG	3+			★			
Hurricane, The	66	R	All	★					
Ice Castles	68	PG	All/1		★		★		
Inconvenient Truth, An	70	PG	All						★
Invincible	71	PG	All/2		★				
K2	73	R	All/2						

Family issues	Health and wellness	History	Inclusion	Leadership	Leisure behavior	Life stages	Outdoor recreation	Physical and mental challenge	Recreation therapy	Sport	Teamwork	Tourism and travel
				★			★	★			★	
					★	★	★					
					★					★		
						★				★		
		★						★		★	★	
★										★	★	
										★		
		★										
		★								★	★	
												★
★		★								★		
					★	★						
				★								
		★		★								★
★		★								★		
			★						★	★		
				★								
				★						★		
				★	★		★	★			★	

(continued)

Title	Page	Rating	Scene selection	Activity	Coaching	Commercial recreation	Competition	Diversity	Environmental issues
Keep Your Eyes Open	75	PG-13	All	★					
League of Their Own, A	77	PG	All/2					★	
Lorax, The	79	G	All						★
Mad Hot Ballroom	81	PG	All/3	★	★		★	★	
Milagro Beanfield War, The	83	R	All/3			★			
Million Dollar Baby	84	PG-13	2		★		★	★	
Miracle	86	PG	All/1		★		★		
Motorcycle Diaries, The	88	R	All/3+						
Moulin Rouge	91	PG-13	1					★	
Mr. Miami Beach: The Remarkable Story of Carl Fisher	92	NR	All			★			
Murderball	94	R	All/2		★		★	★	
My Left Foot	95	R	All/3+						
Mystery, Alaska	97	R	All/3						
Patch Adams	98	PG-13	3+					★	
Project Grizzly	100	NR	All						
Radio	102	PG	All/3		★			★	
Remember the Titans	103	PG	All/3+		★			★	
Ringer, The	105	PG-13	All					★	
River Runs Through It, A	107	PG	All/3+	★				★	
Rize	109	PG-13	All/3+	★			★	★	
Roger & Me	111	R	1			★			

Family issues	Health and wellness	History	Inclusion	Leadership	Leisure behavior	Life stages	Outdoor recreation	Physical and mental challenge	Recreation therapy	Sport	Teamwork	Tourism and travel
					★			★		★		
		★								★		
					★						★	
												★
										★		
				★						★	★	
												★
		★										
												★
								★	★	★		
			★		★			★				
										★	★	
									★			
					★		★	★				
		★								★		
				★	★					★	★	
		★							★			
★		★					★					
					★							
												★

(continued)

Title	Page	Rating	Scene selection	Activity	Coaching	Commercial recreation	Competition	Diversity	Environmental issues
Rookie, The	113	G	All/3+	★	★			★	
Saint Ralph	114	PG-13	All/3+	★	★		★		
Sandlot, The	116	PG	All/3						
Save the Last Dance	118	PG-13	All/3+					★	
Seabiscuit	119	PG-13	All/3+				★		
Searching for Bobby Fischer	121	PG	All/3+		★		★		
Shall We Dance?	123	PG-13	All/3		★		★		
Shot at Glory, A	124	R	All/1		★				
Steel Magnolias	126	PG	All/2						
Super Size Me	127	PG	All/2						
Take the Lead	130	PG-13	All/2	★	★				
Touching the Void	131	R	All/1						
Trekkies	133	PG	All/3+			★			
We Are Marshall	136	PG	All/3		★				
Young and the Dead, The	137	NR	All			★			

Family issues	Health and wellness	History	Inclusion	Leadership	Leisure behavior	Life stages	Outdoor recreation	Physical and mental challenge	Recreation therapy	Sport	Teamwork	Tourism and travel
										★	★	
		★				★						
					★							
		★								★	★	
★					★					★		
					★							
		★								★	★	
★	★				★							
	☆				★							
				★							★	
	★			★			★	★			★	
					★							★
											★	

Preface

A doctor uses laughter to better the lives of his patients in *Patch Adams;* a community fights against development in *The Milagro Beanfield War;* a young boy who wishes for adulthood learns the challenges of it in *Big.* Movies are excellent tools for illustrating the lessons we teach. Concepts such as history, sport, teamwork, and diversity can be better illustrated in the movie *A League of Their Own* than solely through assigned readings.

Teaching With Movies: Recreation, Sports, Tourism, and Physical Education is a resource of pop culture movies. When the films in this book are framed (set up in advance) and debriefed (analyzed afterward) effectively, they can serve as educational tools to enhance learning objectives in a variety of settings. The movie finder on page iv will help you to quickly identify and locate films that meet specific criteria or that fit with certain themes and concepts. On pages 1 to 138, movies are presented alphabetically by title and include the following information:

- Director
- Main actors and actresses
- Year of release
- Rating (along with explanations or cautions, if appropriate)
- Total running time
- Core concepts
- Description of the plot
- Description of specific scenes (if appropriate)
- Framing
- Debriefing
- Concept exploration

The framing section of each entry provides students with the proper perspective for viewing the movie. You can use specific questions to frame an entire film or a specific scene before showing it to your class or group. We also encourage you to use your own favorite framing methods, such as worksheets or lectures.

The debriefing section of each entry provides questions to help students reflect on the connections between the film and the course content. A complement to the framing questions, the debriefing questions are intended to stimulate small-group discussions.

The concept exploration section of each entry provides suggestions for activities to give students a chance to explore aspects of the film's theme in greater depth. We also encourage you to create assignments and projects that are appropriate for your particular class or group.

In short, although we provide guidelines and examples of ways to frame, debrief, and explore the concepts of movies in this book, we don't present an exhaustive, universal list. After all, you know your group better than anyone, and you know what works and what doesn't for your particular class or setting. So, when preparing to show a movie, watch the entire film, consider our suggestions, and gauge the best way to present the material to your audience.

Information about the movies included in this book was obtained from faculty across the United States who participated in a 2005 study conducted by the authors. A total of 67 people responded to an online questionnaire. They were asked to share suggestions about movies they have used successfully and to answer questions about relevant courses, scene selections, and framing and debriefing techniques. Respondents identified nearly 100 movies; the most frequently recommended titles were *The Sandlot*, *Remember the Titans*, and *Super Size Me*. Other common suggestions included *A Class Divided*, *Awakenings*, *Bend It Like Beckham*, *Billy Elliott*, *Hook*, *Miracle*, *My Left Foot*, *One Flew Over the Cuckoo's Nest*, *Patch Adams*, and *Roger & Me*.

The study also showed that movies are used in a variety of classes. Many respondents cited their use of films in introductory courses on recreation, parks, and tourism. Movies were also used in courses related to diversity, inclusion, disabilities, leadership, management, supervision, quality of life, and leisure behavior. Respondents also listed numerous other core concepts, such as women/ethnicity, wilderness leadership, trends, adventure education, assessment, campus recreation, commercial recreation, tourism, legal issues, leisure and contemporary society, wellness, interpretation, philosophy, programming, social psychology, innovation, life spans and aging, stereotypes, decision making, time and work, managing risk, flow, gender roles, prejudice, sexuality, and group dynamics. The results of the study became the foundation for this book, and we incorporated many of the respondents' suggested movies. In addition, we added selections based on our own research.

To develop the 19 core concepts used to categorize the movies in this book, we assembled a master list of topics from all responses to our study and then identified additional topics. A tally was taken to determine how many movies fell into each category. Topics that were underrepresented were deleted from the list, and topics that were similar were combined. This final list gave us a broad framework of core concepts for categorizing the movies.

Not everyone is as knowledgeable about movies as Roger Ebert, Leonard Maltin, or Gene Shalit. Busy professionals in the fields of recreation, sports, tourism, and physical education have little time to research movies to determine which would be appropriate for supplementing their curricula or program topics. Sometimes we're lucky if we can even find time to sit down in a commercial or home theater for two hours!

We, the authors of this book, love to watch movies, but it can be difficult for us to do so without planning lessons in our heads. Our students would tell you we don't show enough movies in class, however. We may show a brief clip to get their attention and then build the lecture and discussion from it. Of course, the students often groan if they don't get to see the whole movie. This can be an advantage, though. It encourages them to rent the movie, watch it on their own time, and make further connections between their coursework and life lessons. *Born Into Brothels* is an excellent example of this. A 10-minute showing in class to prompt discussion on the escape that recreation can provide led to several students viewing the movie on their own time. They participated in spontaneous e-mail discussions about the movie, and a fraternity on campus decided to show the movie as part of a faculty/student panel discussion.

Faculty members often tell their peers about movies they've used successfully with students. However, some as-yet-untenured faculty members may be concerned that the use of pop culture movies in the classroom might appear to reduce rigor and negatively affect their chances of promotion and tenure. But the literature shows that the use of popular culture in the classroom can have a positive effect on students' retention of course information (Fain, 2004). Thus a resource such as *Teaching With Movies* lends legitimacy to the practice of using movies as teaching tools and will benefit both tenured and pre-tenure faculty.

We have found, through discussions with other educators, that there are multitudes of movies people would love to share with their students. Of course, we couldn't include every film that was suitable for use as an educational tool. *Teaching With Movies* is limited by space, not by imagination. Because it is inevitable that you will have ideas for movies not included here or ways to utilize a movie that is included, we have designed a collaborative Web site where you can add to or create new listings for the movie guide. The conclusion of this book explains how to access the Recreation, Sports, Tourism and Physical Education Movies Wiki.

We look forward to sharing these movies with you and hearing your comments about your own success at bringing them into your lessons. Happy viewing and teaching!

Acknowledgments

We would like to thank the following people for their contributions to *Teaching With Movies: Recreation, Sports, Tourism, and Physical Education:*

- Jerusha Greenwood, PhD (California Polytechnic State University, San Luis Obispo)
- Eva Graves (Radford University)
- Breanne Long (California Polytechnic State University, San Luis Obispo)
- James Newman, PhD (Radford University)
- Susan Van Patten, PhD (Radford University)
- Radford University's Managing Travel Resources class, fall 2005

We would also like to thank the following people, who have watched movies and shared popcorn with us:

- Samantha Gill
- Stu and Janie Goldenberg
- Jon Hanlon
- Patrick and Bailey O'Bannon
- Dan Pronsolino
- Lisa and Paul Stagnoli
- Kristi Weddige

Introduction:
Movies as Teaching Tools

Popular culture can be formally defined as art and mass media made popular post 1960. Less formally, popular, or pop, culture pertains to the here and now—what's hot, mainstream, and being talked about around the proverbial water cooler. It includes music, art, entertainment, celebrities, food, drink, and sport. The television show *American Idol* is part of our pop culture, as is musician and actress Madonna, the Harry Potter book series, and the word *dude.*

Contemporary movies that are released to public theaters fall into the category of popular culture. We are inundated by reports of what films are being released, how much money they have earned, and what movie stars are spending their money on. Fast-food chains hype upcoming blockbusters, and television commercials tease us out of our living rooms and into the nearest theater. The Internet has played a major role in the publicity of movies. The 2006 movie *Snakes on a Plane* garnered so much buzz on Web sites and blogs that the script was changed to reflect fan-generated dialogue.

Why are movies so much a part of our popular culture? In the United States, movies are an escape. They give us a glimpse into other lives that we will never experience, such as that of the brave and handsome Indiana Jones or the courageous and magical Harry Potter.

Movies are also part of our social fabric. They illustrate (although not always accurately) history, social movements, and other facets of culture (Turner, 1999). For example, *Gladiator* depicts the Roman era, and *A River Runs Through It* shows life in the early 20th century.

═ MOVIES AS TEACHING TOOLS ═

Movies give us an opportunity to learn in an enjoyable way outside of the traditional classroom environment. Documentaries, such as Al Gore's *An Inconvenient Truth* and Michael Moore's *Roger & Me,* are instructional in a straightforward way. Other movies teach their lessons through metaphor or in other "between the lines" ways. The popular movie *A League of Their Own* can be viewed as a lesson on women's roles in sport history. *Eight Below* is a lesson in leadership, outdoor recreation, and physical and mental challenge.

Movies can be effective teaching tools. A prepared educator can use movies to stimulate discussion, facilitate learning on a particular topic, or reemphasize material being presented through textbooks or classroom lectures. Moving away from straight lecture by showing a movie, especially when pairing it with methods of framing and debriefing, enables an educator to provide a form of active learning that can be very successful (Robinson, 2000). There is a misguided notion that movies are fluff or time wasters and not relevant in the curriculum. Some believe that showing a movie in class is an easy out for the instructor. In reality, there are educational benefits to using movies as teaching tools. They illustrate history, social movements, and many important lessons.

Another benefit to using movies as teaching tools is that they help to humanize the instructor and may lead to enhanced faculty–student interaction (Marshall, 2002; Rogers, 2002). Students are more likely to seek advice and assistance from an instructor who shows an appreciation of popular culture. Having good communication with instructors increases the possibility that students will seek communication with other faculty, thereby leading to a greater degree of success in school (Wilson, 2004). If you have a way to earn students' trust and acceptance, while at the same time facilitating long-term retention of material, use it!

Movies can be shown by recreation, parks, and tourism faculty and instructors, as well as by professionals working in the field. Coaches can use movies to illustrate teamwork, trust, or communication skills to players. They can also use movies to inspire players or help them learn certain skills. A manager of a camp or nonprofit association can use a movie or a scene to illustrate similar topics. After-school programs can also use movies to teach skills or to have the students think about a variety of topics. For example, showing a movie that includes scenes of drug use might encourage youth in an after-school program to participate in a discussion on the subject. (Of course, it is imperative to consider whether the content of a movie is appropriate for your intended audience and to make parents and administrators aware of what you are showing.)

Another group that can benefit from the use of movies as teaching tools is instructors of physical education and exercise science. Movies often portray physical education and physical educators in negative and confusing ways. For instance, physical education teachers are sometimes portrayed as cruel and locker rooms as intimidating. For example, a locker room scene in *Remember the Titans* portrays issues regarding sexuality. Instructors can use these images to address the subject of stereotypes in the field (Duncan, Nolan, & Wood, 2002).

Forms of popular culture other than movies are frequently used as teaching aids. Examples are comic strips, music, and television shows (Marshall, 2002). Clipping a relevant comic strip from the Sunday paper and using it at the start of class is a common way to get students' attention and introduce a topic. Movie scenes can be used in the same way. You do not need to show all two-plus hours of a movie to make a point. Showing a very brief clip from any movie is enough to get most students to sit up and pay attention.

Teachers can also assign movies for students to watch on their own time. This may save formal class time for group discussions. After students view a movie or movie clip, and hopefully complete some sort of activity sheet, they can come to class prepared for a discussion on how the movie relates to the topic discussed in the readings or lecture.

TODAY'S TECHNO-SAVVY YOUTH

Preschoolers are learning to use technology, and as they make their way through the educational and social systems, they are incorporating these skills into everything they do. Today's tweens (9- to 12-year-olds), teenagers, and young adults are highly proficient manipulators of their environments. They have purchasing power and the desire for freedom and personal influence. *Screenagers* is a term being used to identify teens and young adults who are extremely accustomed to digital devices and media input (Rushkoff, 1996). They buy songs from iTunes instead of purchasing a CD at the mall. They IM (instant message) one another on their cell phones, some even using a ringtone that can't be heard by adult ears. Screenagers use Google or Wikipedia for their homework research instead of walking through the stacks in a library. They are habituated to getting information quickly and easily.

Pop culture movies provide a connection between the current generation of learners and educational topics (Marshall, 2002). For example, students can gain an understanding of race relationships in sports from the movie *Remember the Titans*. This understanding can reinforce the topic taught in class. Students are more apt to retain information from lectures and reading if they can relate it to a movie. Imagery is a memory technique that can be used to facilitate long-term memory storage (Davis, 1993). Relating a classroom concept to a movie is a way to provide an association that students can grasp and mentally hold onto in long-term memory. This is especially true for the newest generation of students, who are accustomed to rapid technological changes. Marc Prensky (2001) coined the term "digital natives" to refer to students who have grown up with technology and expect it to be an integral part of their education. Those of us who are trying to catch up and learn how to use technology in our teaching have been dubbed the "digital immigrants" (Prensky, 2001).

Traditional means of teaching and learning don't always hold the attention of young people who are living in such a technology-based, popular culture–worshiping society (Young, 2002). As educators, we must be aware of what motivates our students and determine when supplementary means of imparting knowledge are called for.

MOVIES AS MOTIVATION

Raymond Wlodkowski (1978) researched motivation in teaching. He believed that motivation stimulated behavior, gave direction to behavior, allowed the behavior to continue, and led to the selection of a specific behavior. Wlodkowski believed that motivation was affected by attitudes, needs, stimulation, individual feelings, competence, and reinforcement (Davis, 1993). Teachers are responsible for motivating students using these variables.

Provided that you have sound framing and debriefing, showing a movie addresses the components that lead to motivation. For instance, students generally have positive attitudes about viewing a pop culture movie as part of class. Screenagers' learning needs are often met when a movie in incorporated into their formal education. Watching a movie is certainly stimulating, just as a discussion during the debriefing can be. Students' individual feelings, which make up the classroom climate, will be enhanced when they are told they are going to watch a movie. Competence can be achieved through the concept exploration activities. Reinforcement is entirely up to the instructor, to determine how best to "reward" the students for integrating the movie concepts into their learning.

Consider a professor of recreation, parks, and tourism teaching a class on ethics. She regularly uses pop culture movies in her classroom to give the students opportunities to view ethical conundrums and then to discuss the situations in terms of best practices. On the first day of class, she tells the students that they will be watching movies to augment certain topics in the class. She then sends around a sheet of paper that lists various movies under the topics they best represent. The students vote for the movies they would like to watch as a class. This is the start of the professor's motivation process. She has just given the students some control over their education. This "locus-of-control" technique motivates the students to prepare for the movies by doing the required readings.

LEARNING STYLES

As educators, we need to pay attention to how individual students prefer to learn and determine what we can do to capture their attention, hold it, and leave them having learned something. Movies provide an excellent opportunity to address different types of learners. For example, a visual learner takes in the movie visually, whereas an auditory learner learns from listening to the movie and then to the discussion. When teachers address learning styles through popular culture, students' capacity to learn, understand, and retain information is increased. Visual learners appreciate the moving images. Auditory learners remember the dialogue and the music.

THE POWER OF CELEBRITY

As any teacher or parent knows, a child is more likely to heed the advice of a person who is "somebody." A teacher can lecture on famine in Africa, but students will pay particular attention when a movie star such as Angelina Jolie speaks on the topic in a television special. A parent can explain to a teenager that drugs are dangerous, but learning of a young Hollywood celebrity who has died of an overdose may have a more lasting and profound effect. There is no reason to fight the fact that movies and movie stars hold sway over the populace. In an education setting, we would do well to use it to our advantage.

ORGANIZATION OF TEACHING WITH MOVIES

Each movie in this book is presented using 12 pieces of information: movie title, director, actors starring in the movie, year of release, rating, total running time, core concepts, description of the movie, scenes, framing, debriefing questions, and concept exploration.

Information for *Teaching With Movies* was gathered from a variety of sources. The DVD and video jackets were the most obvious source of facts, such as who directed and starred in the movie. Particular Web sites were very helpful. We frequently used the Internet Movie Database (www.imdb.com), the Classification and Rating Administration's site (www.filmratings.com), and Blockbuster's site (www.blockbuster.com). Some movies have proved so popular that they continue to have devoted Web sites, such as the official *Billy Elliot* site (www.billyelliot.com).

Basic Information

The first part of each movie entry covers basic information about the film.

Title

The formal movie title is provided. Movies are listed in alphabetical order.

Director

This is the name of the person who directed the movie.

Starring

This a list of the main actors who appear in the movie. Students' interest in a film may increase because they recognize the names of some of their favorite stars. This information is not included for documentaries.

Documentary

Most of the films detailed in *Teaching With Movies* are fiction. However, the book includes popular documentaries that address recreation and related themes. If a movie falls into this category, the word *Documentary* appears in place of the list of main actors.

Year

This is the year the movie was released.

Rating

All movie ratings are provided as well as available information on why they are rated a certain way. Before you show a movie, be sure you're aware of the reasons for its rating and whether it is appropriate for your intended audience. Occasionally, the broad term "thematic elements" is given, which means that some aspects of a movie may be potentially upsetting to the audience. Some movies include only the rating and not the reason for the rating. This is generally because the information was not available for older movies.

Running Time

This is the total running time of the movie. Note that the Scenes section also indicates whether you should show the film in its entirety or show just one or a few scenes, depending on their relevance to the theme of recreation and leisure.

Core Concepts

This section lists the most relevant topics addressed in the movie to help you quickly find films that you can use to supplement your learning material. The movies in this book are labeled with the following core concepts: activity, coaching, commercial recreation, competition, diversity, environmental issues, family issues, health and wellness, history, inclusion, leadership, leisure behavior, life stages, outdoor recreation, physical and mental challenge, recreation therapy, sport, teamwork, and tourism and travel.

These core concepts are some of the basic themes that can be explored, but the list is by no means exhaustive. Many of the movies in this book can be used to depict multiple core concepts.

Activity

A number of movies depict recreational activities, including golf, boxing, and dance. The activity itself may be a topic of discussion in the classroom, or it may support other topics such as teamwork or sport. For example, the focus of *Mad Hot Ballroom* is ballroom dancing.

Coaching

Movies that depict coaching are usually related to sports rather than the purely psychological concept of coaching. Various methods and styles of coaching are exemplified. Some coaching methods can be equated to management styles, such as in the movie *The Bad New Bears*.

Commercial Recreation

Commercial recreation refers to providing a service in exchange for a fee. Examples of commercial recreation enterprises are movie theaters, hotels, and bike rental businesses. This is a specific aspect of the field, and only a few movies fit into this concept. Movies with this core concept are suitable for classes in management or commercial recreation. An example is *The Hudsucker Proxy*, in which the lead character demonstrates a passion for innovation.

Competition

Movies that depict this core concept focus on competition between two or more groups of individuals or on competition within one group. For example, *Miracle* looks at the U.S. ice hockey team that went to the Olympics in 1980.

Diversity

The term *diversity* is used to express concepts such as race, ethnicity, social classes, culture, and age. These topics are often part of Introduction to Recreation, Parks, and Tourism classes. Examples of movies with diversity themes are *Save the Last Dance*, in which two young people overcome social stigmas to have an interracial relationship, and *Bend It Like Beckham*, in which a young woman of Indian descent fights her family's expectations of her.

Environmental Issues

An example of a movie in which a specific environmental issue or topic is addressed is *Hoot*. In this film, teenagers use teamwork and determination to save endangered owls.

Family Issues

Movies that include this core concept address themes pertaining to families and relationships. Some movies involve parental involvement or family pressure. An example is the father character in the movie *Billy Elliot*, who is angered by his son's choice of recreation. Family issues must be a central theme of the movie and be relevant to recreation, sports, tourism, or physical education to be linked to this concept. For example, the movie *Failure to Launch* is about a young man at odds with his parents. However, the scenes we recommend are not directly related to that aspect of the movie.

Health and Wellness

Health and wellness issues include obesity (*Super Size Me*), illness, death, and old age (*Cocoon*). These movies often fit well into recreation, sports, tourism, and physical education introductory courses, as well as leisure behavior courses.

History

These movies depict an era in history that is relevant to a class in recreation, parks, and tourism administration. *Gladiator* depicts the Roman era, when people paid to watch men fight for their lives.

Inclusion

Inclusion refers to a duty to ensure that recreation opportunities are available for all people, regardless of ability. Inclusion allows people with special needs to participate in activities at a level they are comfortable with. For example, *The Ringer* depicts the joy of participants in the Special Olympics. An ice skater, blinded in an accident, experiences inclusion in *Ice Castles*.

Leadership

Leadership is distinguishable from coaching in that it addresses issues that are not necessarily related to sport. Coaches are certainly leaders, but there are other forms of leadership as well. Leadership, decision making, and goal setting are focuses for movies with this core concept. Examples include *Eight Below*, in which a guide in the wilderness has to make decisions regarding a research project and the weather, and *Hoot*, in which a boy rallies others around an environmental issue.

Leisure Behavior

Each of us has a unique take on what recreation, leisure, and play mean on a personal level. Many of the movies in this text relate to leisure behavior at their core and are useful for exemplifying a number of more specific topics, such as enjoyment of an activity, dangerous or illegal recreation, sexuality, stereotypes, or other ways people express themselves through leisure. For example, in *Project Grizzly*, Troy Hurtubise spends his leisure time developing a protective suit that will allow him to interact with bears.

Life Stages

From infancy through old age, people experience leisure in various ways. A number of movies exemplify the changes we move through as we age and how life stages affect recreational activities. An example is *The Sandlot*, in which we watch a young boy learning about friendship and baseball as his older self narrates the movie.

Outdoor Recreation

Many movies, such as *Eight Below, K2,* and *The Endurance: Shackleton's Legendary Antarctic Expedition,* show people involved in recreation in outdoor settings. Some of these movies also focus on historical events that affected the outdoor recreation industry.

Physical and Mental Challenge

A person or group facing a challenge is a significant theme in a number of movies. Challenges may be physical or mental in nature. *Keep Your Eyes Open* is an example of a movie in which the participants face both mental and physical challenges.

Recreation Therapy

Like other forms of therapy, recreation can be used as a tool to help people with special needs strive for a healthier, more active life. Recreation therapy is a strong concept in a number of movies, as characters use various forms of leisure to develop their self-confidence and strength, as well as diminish stereotypes. *Murderball* is a wonderful example of athletes finding their strength and passion through the hard-core sport of wheelchair rugby.

Sport

Many movies are focused on sports and sport teams. Some also illustrate teamwork and coaching. *Bend It Like Beckham, The Bad News Bears,* and *Bobby Jones: Stroke of Genius* are just a few of the many movies focused on sports.

Teamwork

Depicting people competing or working together to complete a task are ways that movies use teamwork to illustrate a point. In *Breaking Away,* a group of young men compete in a cycling race in which they are the underdogs.

Tourism and Travel

Many movies show various cultures or people involved with the travel and tourism industry. The movies can be honest (*Roger & Me*), comical (*About Schmidt*), stereotypical (*The Gods Must Be Crazy*), or serious (*The Beach*).

Description of the Movie

The overview for each film includes a brief description for the instructor, an explanation of the relationship of the movie to primary topics, information on scene selection, and warnings about any graphic elements such as violence or sexual content.

Scenes

Some movies are best watched in their entirety; others have particular scenes that illustrate appropriate points. This section describes specific scenes to help you locate them in the movie. It's best to watch the entire movie at least once before showing it to your class or group. This will give you a basic understanding of the premise and help you find suggested scenes.

In the Movie Finder, the following "Scene Selection" codes will help you know how much of a movie is recommended:

- "All" means the movie may be shown in its entirety.
- A number tells you how many specific scenes are appropriate. The code "3+" indicates that there are more than three scenes to choose from.

For example, "All/3" indicates that you should consider showing the entire movie, but if time is limited, you can just show three separate scenes.

Framing

Framing is a way to help students adopt the proper perspective from which to watch the movie. This section provides methods for introducing the class or group to the themes the movie addresses. Methods include group discussion, reading assignments, lectures, and handouts. The method you use will depend on your teaching style, the size of your class or group, the types of learners who will be watching the movie, and other factors. You are certainly not limited to the methods suggested here.

It's important to let students know why you are showing a movie. If they perceive it as a "time waster," they are not going to pay attention, or they will pay attention to irrelevant information. Perhaps they have seen the movie before and have preconceived notions of what the key scenes are. Your job is to help students know the "point" of a movie. How is it relevant to the topic being discussed?

To frame a movie, consider one of the following techniques:

- Ask students what they know about a specific topic. "What do you know about global warming?" is a framing question that would be useful before showing *The Day After Tomorrow*. The question can be used as a large- or small-group discussion prompt or a writing prompt.
- Ask students what they have read about a specific topic. This framing method can be used during the class prior to the movie being shown. Have students locate articles in the popular press (such as newspapers or magazines) on the topic of global warming, for instance.
- Ask students to express how the topic affects them personally. This is an excellent framing technique to use for journaling or other writing assignments. Encouraging personal reflection before seeing the movie will help drive the topic home.
- Framing can also be accomplished through a verbal introduction to the movie's plot and relevance to a topic.

Debriefing Questions

After showing a movie, debriefing activities allow you to help students identify learning concepts and follow up with a discussion and activities. *Debriefing* is another term for evaluation. Examples of evaluation tools are quizzes, small-group discussions, large-group discussions, individual written reactions, lectures, worksheets, and in- or out-of-class reflections. Evaluations can take a few minutes to several hours, depending on the depth of evaluation that is appropriate. During the framing, let the students know there will be a debriefing and what form it will take. We have included debriefing questions for each movie. Use the questions to formulate debriefing exercises that work best for the group you are working with.

To debrief a movie, consider one of the following techniques:

- Have the students write a brief summary of the movie.
- Ask students to write or discuss the key issues that stood out in the movie. Make sure they relate the issues to the class subject or textbook topics.
- As an essay, have the students compare and contrast two or more movies in terms of how they relate to the class subject.
- Ask students to respond in writing or discussion to the following questions: How did the character represent the issue or topic? How can you expand and address in greater detail the topic you saw in this movie? Who would you talk to in order to gain more information on this topic?
- If you had students collect popular press articles on the topic during the framing stage, ask them to compare and contrast the information in the articles with what they saw in the movie. Did they find evidence of global warming effects that were reflected in *The Day After Tomorrow*?

Framing and debriefing are excellent opportunities to address visual and auditory learning styles. Both styles of learners would benefit from groups acting out key roles or developing skits based on a core concept. Have students develop a short film based on a topic related to the one addressed in the movie. Provide handouts so all types of learners have something to hold in their hands, look at, and expand on.

Concept Exploration

This section provides suggestions for advanced learning opportunities and taking concepts from the classroom to the community. Concept exploration may include individual or small-group activities outside the classroom, journaling, and discipline-specific activities tailored to a leisure behavior course. The goal of concept exploration is to extend the learning experience. Giving students an out-of-class assignment related to the movie and its learning concepts makes the movie a stronger tool for learning.

USING THE MOVIE FINDER

You can use the movie finder (see page iv) to browse the list of films in this book to find one that has core concepts that match your planned topic or theme. The movie finder also provides the page numbers on which each film's entry begins.

Remember that the best way to judge whether a movie is suited for your class or group is to watch the entire movie first. This will help you with framing and debriefing and ensure that you use only the most relevant aspects of the movie in your classroom.

=== SUMMARY ===

Students love watching movies. They love the break from regular lectures, the opportunity to sit in a darkened room, and the chance to let their imaginations take flight. As educators, we should love showing movies because they give us an opportunity to capture students' attention and supplement a lesson. Take the time to watch a movie in its entirety before showing scenes to your group. Develop framing methods based on your students' learning styles and educational level. Let students know why you are showing the movie. Ask yourself: If a parent or teacher walked into my classroom while I was showing a movie, how would I justify it? If you use the material presented in this resource well, you will have no problem answering that question. And your students will thank you for it!

13 Going on 30

DIRECTOR: Gary Winick

STARRING: Jennifer Garner, Mark Ruffalo, Judy Greer, Andy Serkis

YEAR: 2004

RATING: PG-13 (some sexual content and brief drug references)

RUNNING TIME: 98 min.

CORE CONCEPTS: Leisure behavior, life stages, activity

Jenna Rink (Jennifer Garner) is a 13-year-old in 1987 who is unhappy with her life and wishes she were 30 years old and popular. Her wish comes true, and she is transported 17 years into the future where she is a successful, sexy, 30-year-old woman. She has to learn to be part of this life and also rectify what she has missed from her past.

SCENES

This movie can be shown in its entirety. A few scenes show Jenna struggling to fit in as a 30-year-old. In one scene that shows leisure behavior, Jenna, now 30, is at a work party and gets everyone dancing to Michael Jackson's "Thriller." Leisure behavior is also depicted when Jenna, at 30, invites 13-year-old girls for a sleepover and they dance on the bed.

FRAMING

Provide some readings on leisure behavior or youth development. Ask questions such as the following:

- ★ What challenges would you face if you were suddenly 17 years older?
- ★ What do you do in your leisure now that you would want to continue in the future?
- ★ How do leisure interests change as we grow older?

DEBRIEFING QUESTIONS

This movie lends itself to discussion on leisure behavior and life stages.

Ask questions such as the following:

* How did Jenna's leisure change throughout the movie?
* What can people do to be youthful?
* What role did leisure play in this movie?
* What leisure activities do people participate in at various stages in their lives?

CONCEPT EXPLORATION

The following activities, assignments, or discussion ideas facilitate concepts from this movie:

* Interview three or four people from various generations and ask them about their leisure interests. Find out how their leisure has changed over the years.
* Interview 13- and 30-year-olds to learn how they are different and how they are similar.
* Watch this movie and compare it to other movies that have similar ideas, such as *Big*. What differences and similarities do you find?

··· NOW PLAYING ···

50 First Dates

DIRECTOR: Peter Segal

STARRING: Drew Barrymore, Adam Sandler, Rob Schneider, Sean Astin

YEAR: 2004

RATING: PG-13 (crude sexual humor and drug references)

RUNNING TIME: 99 min.

CORE CONCEPTS: Recreation therapy, inclusion, health and wellness

Henry Roth (Adam Sandler) is a veterinarian at a marine park in Hawaii. He is a womanizer who is afraid of commitment until he meets Lucy (Drew Barrymore). Lucy was in a major car accident a year earlier and has lost her short-term memory. To protect her, her father and brother act as though each day is the day she got into the accident. Henry pursues her but has to keep having her get to know him all over again each day. He comes up with a plan to help her with her short-term memory, which includes a videotape and her keeping a journal. He falls in love with her, and she loves him as well.

SCENES

You can show the movie in its entirety or just specific scenes. In one scene Henry learns about the accident from Lucy's friends in the restaurant. He then realizes what he is up against, and they encourage him not to get involved. In another scene Lucy has her first hard day with Henry around. Henry learns that Lucy gets very upset when she realizes what has happened to her life. He goes with her and her family back to the doctor and gets a view into her life.

FRAMING

Provide readings on head injuries and how they affect people's choice of recreation and leisure activities. Ask questions such as the following:

* What would it be like to participate in recreation and leisure if you did not remember short-term events?
* How can recreation and leisure professionals program for people with head injuries? Knowing the history of therapeutic recreation, what has changed in the past 20 years? In the past five years?

DEBRIEFING QUESTIONS

Discussion topics can include working with people with physical disabilities and how disabilities affect recreation and leisure. Ask questions such as the following:

* What considerations need to be made when working with people with physical disabilities? Mental disabilities?
* How has therapeutic recreation changed over the years?
* How do families adjust to family members with disabilities? How did Lucy's family adjust to her situation?

CONCEPT EXPLORATION

The following activities, assignments, or discussion ideas facilitate concepts from this movie:

★ Visit people who have head injuries. Work with them for a given length of time. Keep a journal of what you learn. Chart changes in their behavior, as well as changes you may experience personally. Did your personal views and beliefs change? In what way?

★ Make a program plan for people with various physical and mental disabilities. Discuss how programming will vary for people with various needs.

★ Interview people who have family members with disabilities. How has the situation changed their family structure? Did they have to adapt to accommodate this person? In what way? What challenges do they face, and what highlights do they experience?

··· NOW PLAYING ···

About Schmidt

DIRECTOR: Alexander Payne

STARRING: Jack Nicholson, Hope Davis, Dermot Mulroney, Kathy Bates

YEAR: 2002

RATING: R (language and brief nudity)

RUNNING TIME: 125 min.

CORE CONCEPTS: Leisure behavior, life stages, tourism and travel, family issues

Warren Schmidt (Jack Nicholson) retires from a career in which he has worked his entire life. His wife dies suddenly, and he tries to figure out what he will do with his life. His adventures include a road trip in his new RV, his daughter's (Hope Davis) wedding, and a correspondence with a child in Tanzania. His daughter's future mother-in-law (Kathy Bates) is very different in her views of life, and Warren must live with her for a few days and learn to adjust.

SCENES

This movie can be shown in its entirety. If time is limited, two scenes can be shown. The first scene takes place on the first morning of Warren's retirement. His wife is excited about their upcoming adventures, but he is not thrilled. In another scene Warren is in the RV park on his tour and a man comes to visit and "tour" his RV. He invites Warren to dinner in his smaller RV.

FRAMING

Provide readings on stages in the human life cycle or retirement. Ask questions such as the following:

- ★ What are your plans for retirement?
- ★ What leisure activities are you currently involved in that you could do during your leisure time when you retire?

DEBRIEFING QUESTIONS

The movie lends itself to a discussion on leisure behaviors, life stages, and family issues. Ask questions such as the following:

- ★ What issues did Warren face as his life changed?
- ★ How did his retirement plans change?
- ★ What parts of this movie relate to leisure behavior?
- ★ What lifestyles were seen in this movie? How did they vary?
- ★ What roles did family dynamics and family issues play in this movie?

CONCEPT EXPLORATION

The following activities, assignments, or discussion ideas facilitate concepts from this movie:

- ★ Research leisure behavior during retirement. What issues do people face when they retire? What do they hope for in their retirement?
- ★ When families merge through marriage, what challenges do they face? Interview several newly married couples and find out the roles family dynamics and family issues played in their ceremonies and in their lives.

Ali

DIRECTOR: Michael Mann

STARRING: Will Smith, Jon Voight, Mario Van Peebles, Ron Silver, Jeffrey Wright, Mykelti Williamson, Jada Pinkett Smith, Nona Gaye, Jamie Foxx

YEAR: 2001

RATING: R (some language and brief violence)

RUNNING TIME: 159 min.

CORE CONCEPTS: Sport, history, competition

This movie is based on the life of Muhammad Ali (Will Smith). Ali is very bold and outspoken, and after several fights and many struggles and challenges, he becomes the heavyweight champion. This movie depicts Ali's allegiance to the Nation of Islam, his friendship with Malcolm X, and his name change from Cassius Clay to Muhammad Ali. This movie shows Ali's personal life as well, including his refusal to participate in the military draft, which makes him unable to box legally in his own country.

SCENES

If you cannot show this movie in its entirety, show the scene at the end in which Ali fights George Foreman. This scene depicts the challenges and support the two men encounter while fighting in another country.

FRAMING

Provide readings on history and how it affects sport and recreation. Ask questions such as the following:

* What do you know about Malcolm X and the Nation of Islam?
* How do beliefs and culture affect people?
* How much would you sacrifice for your belief?

DEBRIEFING QUESTIONS

This movie lends itself to a discussion on sport, history, and boxing. Ask questions such as the following:

* How did this era in history affect Ali, and how did this affect his recreation and leisure? How did this affect the recreation and leisure of people who were of various races and ethnicities?
* What beliefs did Ali hold that affected his boxing?
* Why is Ali looked up to as a great sport hero?
* What other sport figures are known for their political and religious views? How do politics and religion affect sport?

CONCEPT EXPLORATION

The following activities, assignments, or discussion ideas facilitate concepts from this movie:

* Research the life of Muhammad Ali. Where did he come from? What did he do after the fight with George Foreman?
* Research other sport and recreational activities that occurred during this era. How were they affected by what was going on in the nation?
* What other sport figures are known for their political and religious views? Read about these people and compare their impact with Muhammad Ali's.
* How are sports and politics currently linked? Research current media sources (newspapers and magazines) to find out what is being written about these two topics.

Awakenings

DIRECTOR: Penny Marshall

STARRING: Robin Williams, Robert De Niro, John Heard, Julie Kavner, Penelope Ann Miller, Ruth Nelson

YEAR: 1990

RATING: PG-13 (brief strong language)

RUNNING TIME: 121 min.

CORE CONCEPTS: Recreation therapy, leisure behavior

Based on a true story, this movie takes place in a hospital in the Bronx in 1969. The movie starts with the hiring of Dr. Malcolm Sayer (Robin Williams) to be the doctor for several comatose patients, even though Sayer's background is working in labs. The patients have encephalitis lethargica and have been comatose for several years with no hope of recovery. Dr. Sayer discovers a chemical treatment and gets permission to administer it to one patient. When that patient, Leonard (Robert De Niro), shows outstanding results, Dr. Sayer is able to administer it to more patients. The movie shows these patients experiencing life for the first time in many years and also how their families react to their awakenings.

═ SCENES ═

This movie can be shown in its entirety. A scene at the beginning when Sayer first starts working with the comatose patients includes him using a baseball and then music to get reactions. A few scenes that focus on therapeutic recreation include one in which Leonard goes out of the hospital for the first time to see the area and experience society. He is at a lake and very excited to be in the water. In another scene the entire group travels outside the hospital to experience the world. They first go to a garden and then go dancing. They are extremely happy and enjoying recreation.

FRAMING

Provide some readings on therapeutic recreation, the comatose state, or encephalitis. Ask questions such as the following:

* What would you like to experience if you have been comatose for several years and just awakening?
* What role does therapeutic recreation play in rehabilitation?
* When the events depicted in this movie took place in 1969, how did society view therapeutic recreation? How has this changed throughout the years, and who or what has had a major impact on these changes?

DEBRIEFING QUESTIONS

This movie lends itself to a discussion on therapeutic recreation, comatose patients, or the role of the doctor with people with disabilities. Ask questions such as the following:

* What did the doctor do that was related to therapeutic recreation?
* How has therapeutic recreation changed since 1969?

CONCEPT EXPLORATION

The following activities, assignments, or discussion ideas facilitate concepts from this movie:

* Research encephalitis and learn how it affects people.
* Visit people who are comatose and find out whether therapeutic recreation is used in their lives and how.
* What role did leisure behavior play in this movie? Was it portrayed accurately?
* Read about treatment plans for people who are affected by encephalitis. Investigate the recreation and leisure activities associated with these treatment plans.

The Bad News Bears

DIRECTOR: Michael Ritchie

STARRING: Walter Matthau, Tatum O'Neal, David Pollock, Quinn Smith, David Stambaugh, Brandon Cruz

YEAR: 1976

RATING: PG (language and mature themes)

RUNNING TIME: 102 min.

CORE CONCEPTS: Competition, sport, coaching, teamwork, family issues

Morris Buttermaker (Walter Matthau) is hired to coach a Little League team, the Bears, to avoid a year in jail. The Bears are a group of misfit kids who are not athletic; they are the worst team in the league. Buttermaker must pull himself together to get the team to work together and gain the respect of the players.

SCENES

This movie can be shown in its entirety. If time is limited, consider showing two scenes. In the first, the coach has a conversation with one of the team members after the first game they lose. The boy is up in a tree and Buttermaker tries unsuccessfully to communicate with him. The second scene shows the Bears' competition against the Yankees in the championship game. This scene depicts the pressure of parents on team members and how the team must work together.

FRAMING

Provide some readings on coaching, youth sports, or parental pressure in sports. Ask questions such as the following:

* Have you ever experienced parental pressure while playing a sport?
* How have coaches influenced your choices in recreational activities?
* What struggles have you experienced in youth sports?

═ DEBRIEFING QUESTIONS ═

This movie lends itself to a discussion on sports, youth sports, coaching, teamwork, and parental pressure. Ask questions such as the following:

- ★ What coaching strategies did you see in this movie?
- ★ How did the team come together?
- ★ How would you coach this team?
- ★ In what way does coaching affect a team?
- ★ What role did sports play in the lives of the characters in this movie?

═ CONCEPT EXPLORATION ═

The following activities, assignments, or discussion ideas facilitate concepts from this movie:

- ★ Volunteer to coach a youth sport team. What do you learn about yourself and the sport as a coach? What struggles do you face? Interview coaches of several youth sport teams and discover the type of coaching they use with their teams.
- ★ Attend a youth competition and watch how parents relate to their children and the other parents.
- ★ Watch other movies that show coaching styles, such as *Miracle*, *Bend It Like Beckham,* and *Remember the Titans* and compare and contrast the coaching styles. What parts of each coaching style worked? If you were to coach, which coach would you be the most like and why?

The Beach

DIRECTOR: Danny Boyle

STARRING: Leonardo DiCaprio, Tilda Swinton, Robert Carlyle, Virginie Ledoyen, Guillaume Canet

YEAR: 2000

RATING: R (violence, sexuality, and drug content)

RUNNING TIME: 119 min.

CORE CONCEPTS: Tourism and travel, environmental issues, leisure behavior

A young man named Richard (Leonardo DiCaprio) embarks on an adventure to experience life. He arrives in Thailand and goes out of his way to be anything but the typical American tourist. Richard meets a man who gives him a map to a secret island beach. Richard sets off toward the mysterious island, eventually being joined by two companions. Once on the island, they must fight through a series of barriers, including a fiercely protected marijuana farm. They meet with a group of people who call the isolated beach home. They are led by a woman, Sal, who is very protective of the beach and would rather that others died than reveal the secret to outsiders. Richard ultimately finds that paradise has a price and that he is not willing to pay for it with his life, although it almost comes to that.

═ SCENES ═

The movie can be viewed in its entirety, although several scenes are disturbing. One character commits suicide; others are mauled by a shark. Drugs are very much a part of the story, as is lust. However, specific scenes would be useful. The beginning of the movie, in which Richard narrates his time in Bangkok, shows his desire to find adventure. In scene 4, "An Adventure," Richard and his traveling companions head for the island. Brief scenes of the regular tour routes are shown. Scenes 9 through 13 show Richard's arrival at the beach and his initiation into the group.

An editon of the DVD has a featurette that discusses the movie's themes.

FRAMING

Prepare students for this movie by asking them to pay attention to environmental tourism and cultural tourism issues.

* Explain to students that the movie was filmed on location in Thailand and had a profound effect on the nation's tourism. Young people flocked to the areas where the movie was filmed, including Krabi, Bangkok, Khao Yai National Park, and Phi Phi Leh Island. Some areas experienced environmental degradation as a result of the massive influx of visitors.

* Ask students if there is anything that is ethical and legal that they would not do while visiting another country. In the movie, Richard drinks snake blood and takes drugs (which is legal in some countries).

DEBRIEFING QUESTIONS

This movie lends itself to a discussion on tourism, environmental issues, and leisure behavior. Students may be overwhelmed by the messages in this movie. Help them to focus by asking them the following:

* What do you think of Richard's exploits? Would you ever consider such a wild adventure? How do you think Richard's experience on the island affected the choices he made thereafter?

* Discuss Richard's definition of paradise, which he shares in the last few scenes of the movie. How would you define paradise?

CONCEPT EXPLORATION

The following activities, assignments, or discussion ideas facilitate concepts from this movie:

* Research the full moon beach parties held in Koh Phangan, Thailand. In the movie, Koh Phangan is where the community members trade their marijuana for food, beverages, and other goods. In real life, Koh Phangan hosts one of the wildest parties on the planet. Tourists from around the world flock to this little corner of Thailand to "lose themselves" with thousands of other people.

* Research and describe in writing an adventure trip that would push the limits of your comfort zone.

★ Use the movie as a starting point to discuss the impacts of tourism on the environment. Tourists flocked to Thai beaches after the release of this movie, causing degradation in areas that were not prepared for large numbers of people.

···NOW PLAYING···

Bend It Like Beckham

DIRECTOR: Gurinder Chadha

STARRING: Parminder Nagra, Keira Knightley, Jonathan Rhys Meyers

YEAR: 2003

RATING: PG-13 (language and sexual content)

RUNNING TIME: 112 min.

CORE CONCEPTS: Diversity, family issues, sport, coaching

This movie takes place in England and depicts the struggle of a young woman, Jess (Parminder Nagra), who wants to play football (soccer). Because of their Indian culture and traditions, Jess' parents do not support her or encourage her to play. Jess plays clandestinely on a girls' team. Eventually her father learns what she is doing and accepts and supports her after many struggles around family traditions and her sister's wedding.

═ SCENES ═

This movie can be shown in its entirety, but two scenes illustrate the struggle that Jess faced to play football. In one, she lies to her parents that she is working and then goes to practice. The wedding scene at the end of the movie is also very powerful. Jess is unhappy at the wedding, and her friend wants to sneak her off to play in the last half of the final championship game. Her father overhears and encourages her to go, but only if she has a smile on her face when she returns.

FRAMING

Provide some readings on culture and leisure. Ask questions such as the following:

★ How do cultures affect people's leisure choices?
★ In what ways do religious beliefs affect people's choices of sports and recreation?
★ How are gender stereotypes reinforced in sports?

DEBRIEFING QUESTIONS

This movie lends itself to discussions of sports in the context of culture, religion, and family values. Gender issues are also illustrated in the movie. Ask questions such as the following:

★ In what ways do culture and religion affect people's choices in leisure and recreation?
★ What stereotypes apply to recreation in regard to gender, race, ethnicity, religion, and customs?
★ How did the coaching Jess received affect her choices?

CONCEPT EXPLORATION

The following activities, assignments, or discussion ideas facilitate concepts from this movie:

★ Interview people from various cultural backgrounds, compare their customs, and examine how those customs might affect their participation in particular activities.
★ Did your family traditions ever affect the choices you made? What were these choices? How did you deal with them? What did your friends think?
★ Read about various cultures and then visit these cultures through centers, clubs, or religious organizations. Ask questions related to sports, culture, and religion.

Big

DIRECTOR: Penny Marshall

STARRING: Tom Hanks, Elizabeth Perkins, Robert Loggia, John Heard, Jared Rushton

YEAR: 1988

RATING: PG (language)

RUNNING TIME: 104 min.

CORE CONCEPTS: Leisure behavior, life stages

Josh (Tom Hanks) is a 13-year-old struggling with being young. He makes a wish on a carnival machine and becomes a 35-year-old man. As an adult, he is forced to get a job and an apartment and grow up fast. He meets Susan (Elizabeth Perkins), who is interested in a relationship with him. This movie shows the struggles and challenges that Josh faces and his desire to be 13 again.

═ SCENES ═

This movie can be shown in its entirety. If time is limited, two scenes illustrate leisure behavior. In the first, Josh is in a toy store after being an adult for one week and having a full-time job. He is playing with the kids and having a great time. His boss is also there and is checking out how the kids play with toys. They have a good conversation and end up playing a large piano with their feet. Josh's boss promotes him to help with the product development of toys. In the second scene, Susan is interested in Josh. He is happy to have her come up to his apartment and play with him, but they both interpret "play" very differently. They end up jumping on the trampoline, and she sleeps in the bottom bunk.

═ FRAMING ═

Provide some readings on the stages of the life cycle and recreation or leisure behavior across generations. Ask questions such as the following:

★ What recreational activities would you pursue if you were a different age?

* How do stages of development affect people's recreational choices?
* If you suddenly became 20 years older, what recreational activities would you hope you would continue doing?

DEBRIEFING QUESTIONS

This movie can lend itself to a discussion of leisure behavior. Ask questions such as the following:

* What characteristics did Tom Hanks use to portray a 13-year-old?
* How did the character of Josh change throughout the movie?

CONCEPT EXPLORATION

The following activities, assignments, or discussion ideas facilitate concepts from this movie:

* Visit a park or other public place and observe people at various stages in their lives. Compare your observations to a reading you have discussed in class.
* Interview people from three or four generations. Ask them about their recreational patterns, behaviors, and interests. Compare how much money and time they spend on recreation each day or week.

· · · NOW PLAYING · · ·

Billy Elliot

DIRECTOR: Stephen Daldry

STARRING: Jamie Bell, Julie Walters, Gary Lewis, Jamie Draven

YEAR: 2000

RATING: R (strong language)

RUNNING TIME: 111 min.

CORE CONCEPTS: Activity, family issues, diversity, leisure behavior

A young boy fights against gender stereotypes to pursue his dream of dancing ballet. The story follows Billy (Jamie Bell) as he drops his boxing lessons to study ballet with a group of girls. He must sneak and lie to follow his passion. Eventually, Billy's talent can't be hidden. An understanding teacher prods him to audition for the Royal Ballet School. His much-less-understanding father takes longer to see the talent in his son. In the end, Billy attends the school and becomes a lead dancer in a recital his father is proud to see.

SCENES

The movie should be shown in its entirety to fully understand Billy's character, his relationship with his father, and his passion for ballet. Compare scenes of Billy dancing out his anger to those of Kevin Bacon doing the same in *Footloose*. In one scene Billy is in front of an admissions board at a ballet school and he is asked to describe how he feels when he is dancing. This is an excellent scene to use to describe the recreation theory of flow. Be aware that the movie contains some very strong language.

FRAMING

To prepare students for this movie, distribute index cards and ask students to write their gender at the top. Then have them write whether they have taken dance classes at any point in their lives. Why or why not? On the opposite side, ask them to describe what type of "nonperformance" dancing they do. Do they go to clubs or dance to music when they are cleaning the house?

DEBRIEFING QUESTIONS

During the movie, review the response cards with the students' comments. After the movie, share some of the responses with the class, without identifying the writers.

* How many of each gender have taken dance classes? How many males participate in nonperformance dancing?
* Ask students to respond to the results. Are they surprised?
* Ask students if they can explain flow in relation to Billy's feeling while dancing.

CONCEPT EXPLORATION

The following activities, assignments, or discussion ideas facilitate concepts from this movie:

★ Invite a local dance teacher to class. Ask the teacher how dance became his or her vocation. How does the teacher know whether a student has potential, as Billy did? Ask the teacher to describe how he or she feels while dancing. Is it flow? Invite the teacher to instruct the class in some steps from a variety of dance styles, such as ballet, hip-hop, swing, and salsa.

· · · NOW PLAYING · · ·

Bobby Jones: Stroke of Genius

DIRECTOR: Rowdy Herrington

STARRING: James Caviezel, Claire Forlani, Jeremy Northam, Connie Ray, Brett Rice, Malcolm McDowell

YEAR: 2004

RATING: PG (language)

RUNNING TIME: 129 min.

CORE CONCEPTS: Activity, sport, competition, family issues

This movie is inspired by the true story of Bobby Jones, one of the most talented and gifted golfers of the early 1900s. Bobby (James Caviezel) has challenges to face as he learns to control his temper and deal with a disabling illness. At the age of 28, he becomes the only person to have won the Grand Slam, all four amateur competitions. The movie is about his life, his relationship with his parents and grandfather, and the devotion and support of his wife.

SCENES

This movie can be shown in its entirety; if time is limited, several scenes can be used. In the first scene, at Bobby's first amateur competition, other golfers comment that it is embarrassing to play with a kid in the tournament. In another scene, Bobby arrives home from the amateur competition, and the entire town is at the train station to greet him even though he did not win. His parents hug him and the town cheers. His dad, however, pressuring his son, says he will win from now on in front of the entire crowd. In another scene, Bobby wins his third championship competition and is asked if he will become a professional and make money. He responds that he is an amateur. A discussion ensues about how money will ruin sports.

═ FRAMING ═

Provide readings on amateur golf competition, the history of golf, or pressures placed on competitors. Ask questions such as the following:

- ✶ What pressures are placed on competitors in sports?
- ✶ What is the difference between amateur and professional sports?

═ DEBRIEFING QUESTIONS ═

This movie lends itself to a discussion on sports and golf, competition, and family issues. Ask questions such as the following:

- ✶ What pressures does Bobby Jones face throughout his life? How does he deal with these pressures?
- ✶ What has money done to professional sports?
- ✶ How does family pressure and support influence players?

═ CONCEPT EXPLORATION ═

The following activities, assignments, or discussion ideas facilitate concepts from this movie:

- ✶ Research amateur and professional golf and learn which golfers have influenced and changed the sport. How has the sport changed over time? How has the role of women or minorities affected golf competitions? Compare this movie to others about the history of golf such as *A Gentleman's Game* or *The Greatest Game Ever Played*. (You can find other golf movies at www.golfmovies.com.)
- ✶ How does amateur and professional competition affect players and their families in sports such as basketball, football, and soccer? How does competition affect Olympic athletes?

Born Into Brothels: Calcutta's Red Light Kids

DIRECTORS: Zana Briski, Ross Kauffman

DOCUMENTARY

YEAR: 2004

RATING: R (some sequences of strong language)

RUNNING TIME: 83 min.

CORE CONCEPTS: Leisure behavior, diversity, family issues

This documentary tells the experiences of photographer Zana Briski, who spent a considerable amount of time in the red light district of Calcutta, India. Briski lived with prostitutes and their families in brothels for an extended period. She quickly became attached to the children of the prostitutes, who had extraordinary challenges in life. The children were fascinated with Briski's camera, so she decided to teach them about photography. Some of the children had a wonderful aptitude for photography, as the camera lens caught the tragedies and joys in their lives. Along with teaching them, she tried to get the children away from the brothels and into boarding schools.

The children offer a unique perspective of leisure as a means of escape. Often, while their mothers work, the children climb to the roofs of the brothels and fly kites, play games, sing, and dance. They use their imaginations and try to enjoy the space and lives they have. Photography is a recreational activity as well as a learning experience. It gives the children something to do, while promoting happiness in their lives.

Born Into Brothels is certainly not a "feel good" movie. Viewers will find that the plight of the children weighs heavy on their hearts. However, the movie won an Academy Award in 2005 for Best Documentary, and it also received 12 other international awards.

═ SCENES ═

If possible, show the movie in its entirety. If time is a factor show the movie from the beginning through scene 4 ("Photos by Kochi"). These opening scenes really show the children enjoying themselves, how photography is an escape from their lives, and how it gives them a way to find beauty in their surroundings. There are several scenes where the adults beat the children, yell obscenities at them, and insult other adults. These difficult scenes give people an idea of how these children are raised and what they have to go through each day. Scenes 15 and 16 show the children at an exhibition of their photographs and being interviewed by the press. These scenes reveal how excited these children were to show their work to the world.

═ FRAMING ═

Start off by describing the premise of the movie and share your understanding that it isn't an easy thing to watch. Next, consider how you want the students to mentally approach the movie. Have students take notes as they are watching the movie. For instance:

* Focus on the recreational opportunities available and provided for the children. What do they do for fun?
* Consider more recreation/sport/physical education options that could be made available to the children. How?
* Observe how the photography positively affects the children's lives.

═ DEBRIEFING QUESTIONS ═

Immediately after watching the movie, have students move into small groups and discuss their general impressions. Then give them more specific discussion points, such as the following:

* Do these children have recreation?
* Do they feel entitled to recreation?
* Is photography a recreational activity?
* Why did the girls feel embarrassed to use the cameras out in the street? (They lived in such a low income area, people would harass them.)

═ CONCEPT EXPLORATION ═

The following activities, assignments, or discussion ideas facilitate concepts from this movie:

* The plight of the children in Calcutta, India, is not limited to that city or country. Where else and in what way can you envision children in need of a "childhood"?

- ★ Look into organizations that work to provide play to children in need, such as Kaboom! (www.kaboom.org), the American Association for the Child's Right To Play (www.ipausa.org), and the International Play Association (www.ipaworld.org).
- ★ Learn more about the children featured in the movie, and the organization that grew from Briski's efforts, by visiting the Web site Kids with Cameras (www.kids-with-cameras.org). Your students can even send e-mails to these talented, brave children.

···NOW PLAYING···

Breaking Away

DIRECTOR: Peter Yates

STARRING: Dennis Christopher, Barbara Barrie, Paul Dooley, Dennis Quaid, Daniel Stern, Jackie Earle Haley

YEAR: 1979

RATING: PG (language)

RUNNING TIME: 100 min.

CORE CONCEPTS: Sport, teamwork, competition

Four friends (Dennis Christopher, Dennis Quaid, Daniel Stern, and Jackie Earle Haley) in Indiana come from families whose fathers worked or work in the rock quarries. They are nicknamed the Cutters after stonecutters. One of the friends has won a bike and trained to win many local competitions. He looks up to the Italian team, and he becomes disillusioned when he takes part in the team's "cheating" to win the race. The group of friends must come together to face the college students in a bike competition that the entire community supports.

═ SCENES ═

This movie can be shown in its entirety. If time is limited, show the last scene, in which the Cutters pull together in the college bike race. The first scene of the movie shows the background of the town and the unstructured leisure of hanging out and swimming in the quarry.

FRAMING

Provide some readings on unstructured leisure or challenges groups face with stereotypes. Ask questions such as the following:

* What stereotypes have you faced in your life? How has that affected your leisure choices?
* Have you ever had to pull together as a team to overcome an obstacle? What happened?

DEBRIEFING QUESTIONS

This movie lends itself to a discussion on sports and teamwork. Debriefing questions can include the following:

* What stereotypes did you see in this movie?
* How did this group come together to take part in the competition?
* What does competition do for a group of people?

CONCEPT EXPLORATION

The following activities, assignments, or discussion ideas facilitate concepts from this movie:

* Attend a bike race and observe how the teams work together. What do you notice about teamwork and communication? Relate this to theories and models of teamwork and communication skills.
* Examine other similar team sports and then interview a team that competes together. What struggles do they face? What motivates them to participate in a team activity?

Cars

DIRECTORS: John Lasseter, Joe Ranft

STARRING: (the voices of) Owen Wilson, Paul Newman, Bonnie Hunt

YEAR: 2006

RATING: G

RUNNING TIME: 116 min.

CORE CONCEPT: Tourism and travel

*C*ars is an animated movie that tells the story of a heady race car who finds himself stuck in Radiator Springs, a dying town on Route 66. The race car, Lightning McQueen, wants nothing to do with the "backward" locals he meets, with the exception of a sexy Porsche named Sally. An old Hudson Hornet named Doc wants Lightning McQueen to leave town, but the locals convince Doc to help keep McQueen there to make some road repairs. While he is in "custody," McQueen learns to see past his stereotypes of the locals and learns more about what is special about their little town.

SCENES

Show scenes 21 through 23. In scene 21, Lightning and Sally take a drive through the beautiful scenery near Radiator Springs. This depicts the natural resources that once attracted tourists. Scene 22 shows how a once-vibrant hotel now sits in shambles. Scene 23 depicts Radiator Springs as a once-active tourist stop on Route 66. Sally explains that the road used to move with the land and was part of the traveling experience. When Interstate 40 was built, bypassing Radiator Springs, the tourists stopped coming. This scene exemplifies how poor tourism planning and development impacts small towns. Lightning sums up the tourists' loss when he says, "They don't even know what they're missing."

FRAMING

Most likely, your students are already familiar with this movie, so you won't need to spend much time framing. Tell the students that you will only be watching a few scenes. Ask them to watch the clips and think about why they are relevant to what you are teaching (tourism planning/development).

⹀ DEBRIEFING QUESTIONS ⹀

Point out to your students that Route 66 and Interstate 40 are actual roads, and real towns experienced losses similar to the fate of the fictional Radiator Springs. The interstate bypass was inevitable due to the increased use of cars and interstate transportation. Therefore, ask your students to consider the following:

* What could the town of Radiator Springs have done to draw immediate visitors from the new interstate? Be creative.
* Share examples of how other small towns have devised ways to increase tourism. Use the Web site Roadside America (www.roadsideamerica.com) to find unusual attractions.

⹀ CONCEPT EXPLORATION ⹀

Take the discussion from fantasy to reality. The following activities, assignments, or discussion ideas facilitate concepts from this movie:

* Identify small towns in your region, state, or even along Route 66 that are in need of renewing tourism due to lack of visitors. Assign an in-depth project where students research such a community and develop ways to increase tourism.
* The movie *Honky Tonk Freeway* (1981) depicts residents of a small town dealing with similar problems to those of the residents of Radiator Springs. If you can find the movie, it would make a fun comparison.
* If you have the time, you may want to treat the students to scene 28, which shows the residents of Radiator Springs fixing up the town, and scene 32, in which the town enjoys renewed interest from tourists (due to celebrity-induced tourism).

Coach Carter

DIRECTOR: Thomas Carter

STARRING: Samuel L. Jackson, Ashanti, Robert Ri'chard, Rob Brown, Rick Gonzalez

YEAR: 2005

RATING: PG-13 (violence, sexual content, language, teen partying, and some drug material)

RUNNING TIME: 136 min.

CORE CONCEPTS: Sport, coaching, teamwork, competition

This movie is inspired by the life of Ken Carter (Samuel L. Jackson), a controversial and talented high school basketball coach who believes his players are students first and athletes second. He benches his undefeated team when they do not perform academically as well as they committed to in a contract. The team, school, and community are all upset, but Carter's actions prove to be lifelong lessons for the team members.

SCENES

The movie can be shown in its entirety. If time is limited, the beginning of the movie shows Ken Carter being offered the job as basketball coach for his former high school. This scene shows his background, how he currently lives, and the condition of the high school team. In another scene Coach Carter sets down the rules and tells the team that in order to play, they must sign his contract.

FRAMING

Provide some readings on coaching, sports and stereotypes, or teamwork. Ask questions such as the following:

★ What would it be like to go back and coach for your high school sport team?

★ Has someone else's belief in you influenced or shaped your life? In what way?

DEBRIEFING QUESTIONS

This movie lends itself to a discussion on sports, coaching, and competition. Ask questions such as the following:

⋆ How did Coach Carter change the lives of his students? How can other people affect a community in this capacity?

⋆ How do sports and recreation influence and change people's lives?

CONCEPT EXPLORATION

The following activities, assignments, or discussion ideas facilitate concepts from this movie:

⋆ Research and write a report on youth who have been influenced by their sport or activity. What did they go through to get there? How did their family and friends support them? Who coached them, and how did this work?

⋆ Compare the coaching style in this movie to the styles in other movies that involve coaching.

⋆ Visit a school that is similar to the one in the movie. Talk to the coaches and the athletes. What struggles do they face? To what do they owe their success?

Cocoon

DIRECTOR: Ron Howard

STARRING: Don Ameche, Wilford Brimley, Hume Cronyn, Jessica Tandy, Maureen Stapleton

YEAR: 1985

RATING: PG-13 (language and sexual references)

RUNNING TIME: 117 min.

CORE CONCEPTS: Life stages, health and wellness, leisure behavior

Cocoon is a great blend of science fiction and portrayals of old age. The theme of the movie is taking risks. Three old men find that their favorite pool has developed some invigorating properties after a group of strangers place "pods" in it. The men go from aging residents of a retirement home to childlike, healthy men with a lust for life. The pods turn out to be alien cocoons with healing powers. The movie shows the stereotypes, as well as the realities, of old age. It also depicts the power of leisure to help people feel young. In the end, a group of people opt to leave Earth and live for eternity on another planet. It's a wonderful analogy for appreciating life.

═ SCENES ═

Cocoon is a fun movie to watch in its entirety. There are some key scenes that support the core concepts. Scene 2, "The Home," shows the lead characters in the retirement home and swimming in the pool, which plays a key role in the story. The dialogue includes some brief, mild references to sex and body parts. Scene 4, "Taking a Risk," shows the men swimming in the pool once the mysterious pods are placed in it. Scene 6, "Come Dancing," shows the men and their wives enjoying themselves dancing. One of the best scenes in the movie is "Why Stay" (scene 13), in which Benjamin (Wilford Brimley) explains to his grandson why he and his wife are going away.

FRAMING

Provide readings or other materials and then ask students the following questions:

- ★ What does it means to be old? Describe stereotypes of old people. Do senior citizens have sex? Are their bodies fragile? Do they live to play bingo?
- ★ Can you picture yourself at age 80? What types of leisure might you experience at that age?

DEBRIEFING QUESTIONS

This movie lends itself to a discussion on old age and life stages, health, and leisure behavior. Ask questions such as the following:

- ★ What stereotypes about old age did the characters in the movie shatter?
- ★ Can the alien storyline and the residents' departure for outer space be an analogy for death?
- ★ Have students find popular press articles about senior citizens doing something active or that shatters stereotypes about age.
- ★ Ask students to create a collage made from advertisements that show active seniors. What are the advertisements promoting?

CONCEPT EXPLORATION

The following activities, assignments, or discussion ideas facilitate concepts from this movie:

- ★ Watch the movie at a local retirement center with the residents. Then take part in small-group discussions about the movie.
- ★ Write your own obituary.

The Cutting Edge

DIRECTOR: Paul Michael Glaser

STARRING: D.B. Sweeney, Moira Kelly, Roy Dotrice, Terry O'Quinn, Michael Hogan

YEAR: 1992

RATING: PG (thematic elements)

RUNNING TIME: 101 min.

CORE CONCEPTS: Sport, coaching, teamwork, competition

The Cutting Edge is a movie about a talented but spoiled figure skater, Kate Moseley (Moira Kelly), who has just lost the 1988 Olympics because she fell during a partner lift. The movie also shows Doug Dorsey (D.B. Sweeney), an ice hockey player, who loses his Olympic dream as well in the 1988 games. After several partners do not work out, Kate's coach finds Doug and asks him to skate with Kate. Resistance and lots of hard work are involved in their training for the national championships and then the Olympics. Throughout the movie the two characters struggle with competition and experience a budding romance. They make it to the Olympics and end up in a relationship as well, overcoming personality differences and stereotypes as they learn to work as a team.

═ SCENES ═

The movie can be shown in its entirety. If time is limited, show the scene in which Doug returns to his family and explains that he has been away training as a figure skater. His brother owns a bar and the people in the bar are friends and family. Because of the stereotypes many have about male figure skaters (such as that male skaters are effeminate, gay, or not "real" athletes), he does not look forward to sharing this information with his family.

═ FRAMING ═

Provide some readings on the Olympics, the pressure of sports and winning, or competition. Ask questions such as the following:

* Were you ever pressured to win at any cost?

* Have you ever stopped enjoying a sport because of the degree of competition?

DEBRIEFING QUESTIONS

This movie lends itself to a discussion on ice skating, teamwork, and competition. Ask questions such as the following:

* What stereotypes did you see these characters facing? How did they deal with them?
* How does the pressure to win affect the characters in the movie?
* What strategies were used for coaching the two skaters?

CONCEPT EXPLORATION

The following activities, assignments, or discussion ideas facilitate concepts from this movie:

* Compare and contrast several movies related to sports and the Olympics in regard to the pressure on the competitors or the various coaching styles.
* Research an Olympic athlete and learn about how the person trained and competed to reach the Olympics. What challenges did the person face? What sacrifices did he or she make to be able to perform at such a high level?
* Interview coaches about their styles of coaching, and compare those styles to the style depicted in the movie.
* Try a new sport, such as figure skating. What do you learn to appreciate about the people who compete in the sport?

The Day After Tomorrow

DIRECTOR: Roland Emmerich

STARRING: Dennis Quaid, Jake Gyllenhaal, Ian Holm, Emmy Rossum, Sela Ward

YEAR: 2004

RATING: PG-13 (intense situations of peril)

RUNNING TIME: 124 min.

CORE CONCEPTS: Environmental issues, physical and mental challenge

Global warming triggers the onset of a new Ice Age. The entire Northern Hemisphere is left under ice after a massive storm hits. Everyone has to wait the storm out or flee south to survive. A climatologist has to make his way through the terrible storm to save his son and a small group of survivors in the New York City Public Library. Ultimately, many American survivors end up being sheltered in Latin American countries.

This movie shows the impact of pollution and burning fossil fuels on the environment. The focus is on the need to act to save future generations from paying the price.

SCENES

This movie is best watched in its entirety, because dialogue throughout discusses the cause of the severe weather. If time is short, consider showing the movie up to the scene in which a ship drifts into the middle of New York City, then move forward to the end scenes where the president thanks Southern Hemisphere countries. In these last scenes, the viewer learns what happened to the geography and population of the Northern Hemisphere.

FRAMING

Provide recent news articles and texts of speeches that describe the physical effects of global warming. Help students separate fact from myth. Ask questions such as the following:

* What do you know about global warming?
* What recreational activities contribute to environmental degradation?

DEBRIEFING QUESTIONS

This movie lends itself to a discussion on environmental issues and physical and mental challenges. Ask questions such as the following:

★ Do you see any similarities between the current, real-world global warming problems and what happened in the movie? Where do we go from here?

★ For tourism students: How would tourists react to a poststorm Earth? Would there be cold and warm weather recreation areas?

CONCEPT EXPLORATION

The following activities, assignments, or discussion ideas facilitate concepts from this movie:

★ For one week, keep track of how many times you take part in activities that pollute the environment, such as smoking, driving a car, or using non-environmentally friendly products. After keeping a record of these activities, write a short paper about your pollution habits and how much of an impact you believe each one has on the environment.

★ Write a letter of concern regarding global warming to a politician representing your district or state. (The teacher should provide the names and addresses of appropriate politicians.)

···NOW PLAYING···

Dirty Dancing

DIRECTOR: Emile Ardolino

STARRING: Jennifer Grey, Patrick Swayze, Jerry Orbach, Cynthia Rhodes, Jack Weston, Jane Brucker, Kelly Bishop

YEAR: 1987

RATING: PG-13 (adult situations and language)

RUNNING TIME: 100 min.

CORE CONCEPTS: Activity, family issues, diversity

This movie takes place in the summer of 1963 when Baby (Jennifer Grey) and her family go to the Kellerman Family Camp. As Baby becomes friends with the entertainment staff, she is exposed to the realities of their lives. She agrees to stand in for one of the dancers who is recovering from an abortion, and Johnny Castle (Patrick Swayze) teaches her the routine. Baby learns about life, love, and dancing, as well as how to respect others.

SCENES

Several scenes in the movie illustrate family camp, dancing, and economic social classes. The issue you would like to address should determine the scene you select. For example, when the family first arrives at the camp, they are immediately signed up for dance lessons. This scene also shows the other camp attendees. Social and economic class differences are depicted in the scene in which the director talks to the wait staff about how they will meet the customers' needs.

FRAMING

Provide readings on family camps and their benefits or economic class differences. Ask questions such as the following:

- ★ Have you ever been to a family or youth camp? What did you learn there?
- ★ In what situations have you been where you have noticed an economic class difference?

DEBRIEFING QUESTIONS

Questions may include issues related to camp experiences, dancing as a form of communication, or economic differences between owners and workers.

- ★ How does this movie depict family camps? Is this accurate?
- ★ How might dancing influence a person's personal expression?
- ★ What other forms of recreation and leisure do people participate in as a form of expression?

CONCEPT EXPLORATION

The following activities, assignments, or discussion ideas facilitate concepts from this movie:

- ★ Research the history of camps. Who started the first camp or family camp? How have camps changed over the years? What struggles and challenges do camps face? What are the various types of camps that exist today, and what sorts of recreation and leisure opportunities are provided at these camps?

★ Interview people who work at camps and find out about their recreation and leisure activities. What do they enjoy about their jobs, and what challenges do they face?

··· NOW PLAYING ···

The Dream Team

DIRECTOR: Howard Zieff

STARRING: Michael Keaton, Christopher Lloyd, Peter Boyle, Stephen Furst, Dennis Boutsikaris

YEAR: 1989

RATING: PG-13 (thematic elements)

RUNNING TIME: 113 min.

CORE CONCEPTS: Recreation therapy, teamwork

Four patients (Michael Keaton, Christopher Lloyd, Peter Boyle, and Stephen Furst) in a psychiatric hospital in Trenton, New Jersey, have all recently been taken off their medications. Their doctor (Dennis Boutsikaris) gets permission to take them to a baseball game, and they head into New York City. During a stop along the way, the doctor witnesses a murder and then gets beaten up. The four men go on their own to New York and face their past lives separately, eventually ending up back together. They deal with all sorts of situations in an attempt to get the doctor out of the hospital.

═ SCENES ═

We encourage showing the first part of the movie, which includes the men going to a group session and the doctor getting permission to take the men to the baseball game. His supervisor questions this plan and asks how a ball game can serve as therapy.

FRAMING

Provide readings on therapeutic recreation and working with patients with psychiatric illnesses or mental disabilities. Ask questions such as the following:

* What is therapeutic recreation?
* How can therapeutic recreation be used with people with psychiatric illnesses or mental disabilities?
* What are the benefits of therapeutic recreation?
* How has the use of therapeutic recreation changed over the years?

DEBRIEFING QUESTIONS

The movie lends itself to a discussion on therapeutic recreation and how people with disabilities can benefit from participating in therapeutic recreation. Ask questions such as the following:

* How has therapeutic recreation affected these men?
* How has therapeutic recreation changed over time?
* How has therapeutic recreation affected people you know or have met?
* What activities can be used for people with various disabilities?

CONCEPT EXPLORATION

The following activities, assignments, or discussion ideas facilitate concepts from this movie:

* Develop a therapeutic recreation plan for people with mental disabilities or psychiatric illnesses. Plan for an individual and for a group.
* Visit a psychiatric hospital. Work with patients or interview people who work with patients. What programs work, and how do patients respond to therapeutic recreation?
* Read several articles related to therapeutic recreation and compare them.
* Research the certifications needed to be a therapeutic recreation specialist. How much schooling is required? Can anyone obtain this certification?

Eight Below

DIRECTOR: Frank Marshall

STARRING: Paul Walker, Bruce Greenwood, Moon Bloodgood, Jason Biggs, Gerard Plunkett

YEAR: 2006

RATING: PG (some peril and brief mild language)

RUNNING TIME: 120 min.

CORE CONCEPTS: Leadership, outdoor recreation, physical and mental challenge

This movie is inspired by a true story about a research station in the Antarctic and a dog team and its trainer. The movie starts with the trainer, Jerry Shepard (Paul Walker), taking a researcher out to collect a rock sample. Because of a major winter storm, the researchers at the station radio Jerry and the researcher to return to the station. The weather forces everyone to evacuate the station quickly, and they must leave the eight sled dogs behind. The story focuses on Jerry's efforts to get back to pick up the dogs and the dogs' struggle to survive alone in the Antarctic.

SCENES

This movie can be shown in its entirety. If time is limited, two scenes illustrate the importance of decision making in an outdoor guiding situation. In one, Jerry and the dogs have to pull the sled and the researcher out of a crevasse. Jerry tells the researcher they should not have gone on the expedition. The researcher responds that Jerry, as the guide, should have made the decision to cancel the trip if he had felt it was unsafe; he should not have acquiesced to his boss. In another scene the researcher and Jerry are preparing to start collecting data. They get word from the base that a major storm is approaching and that they should return to the base. However, the researcher convinces Jerry to stay for a half a day more so he can collect his rock sample. This decision leads to a series of incidents from which the story evolves.

FRAMING

Provide readings on outdoor leadership, judgment, decision making, or Antarctic expeditions. Ask questions such as the following:

* How does decision making as an outdoor leader affect outcomes in the wilderness context?
* What decision-making models can you use when you have to make a decision in an outdoor situation?

DEBRIEFING QUESTIONS

This movie lends itself to a discussion on outdoor recreation, leadership, and physical and mental challenges. Ask questions such as the following:

* What challenges did Jerry face in this movie?
* What role does teamwork play in this movie?
* What "human" personalities did the dogs display when they were alone in Antarctica?
* How do a leader's judgment and decision making affect situations in a wilderness setting?

CONCEPT EXPLORATION

The following activities, assignments, or discussion ideas facilitate concepts from this movie:

* Research the story that inspired this movie. Investigate the decision-making process of the guide and how that influenced the outcome of the story.
* Visit or learn about dog sled teams. What struggles do they have? How many working teams exist in a specific state or area? In what ways do the dogs exhibit leadership? How do the dogs and humans work as a team?
* Interview outdoor leaders and find out what decisions they have had to make in the wilderness. How have these decisions affected their trip? In retrospect, what decisions do they wish they had made differently?
* Read about a variety of outdoor expeditions and examine the issues their leaders face. What kinds of judgments and decisions must these leaders make?

The Endurance: Shackleton's Legendary Antarctic Expedition

DIRECTOR: George Butler

DOCUMENTARY

YEAR: 2000

RATING: G

RUNNING TIME: 97 min.

CORE CONCEPTS: Outdoor recreation, leadership, physical and mental challenge, teamwork

This documentary is based on a book that was written about the 1914 Sir Ernest Shackleton Antarctic expedition. The goal was to be the first expedition to cross the Antarctic continent and arrive at the South Pole. The film includes photos from the actual expedition and gives a detailed account of what happened. Of the over 5,000 men who responded to a newspaper ad, Shackleton selected 27 to join him on his expedition. Over the course of months, they sailed until their boat became trapped in the ice. When Shackleton realized that his original goal was impossible to attain, the goal changed to the survival of the crew. The film tells the remarkable story of this expedition.

SCENES

This movie should be shown in its entirety. The documentary provides details about the hardships and challenges that the crew faced in the Antarctic.

FRAMING

Provide some readings on wilderness leadership. Ask questions such as the following:

★ What are the characteristics of an effective leader?

★ How do leaders get followers to work with them?

★ What are some expeditions you have participated in?

★ What types of leadership have you seen in various settings?

DEBRIEFING QUESTIONS

This movie lends itself to a discussion on leadership and wilderness expeditions. Ask questions such as the following:

* How does leadership affect a group's goals?
* What leadership style did Shackleton use?
* How would you deal with the hardships and struggles this group faced?
* What kinds of hardships have you had to face in your life?
* What are some wilderness survival techniques?

CONCEPT EXPLORATION

The following activities, assignments, or discussion ideas facilitate concepts from this movie:

* Interview various leaders who take people into the wilderness. What leadership styles do they use? Are there situations in which they would change their leadership style?
* What is your personal philosophy of leadership? Write a paper on leadership styles and the Shackleton expedition, including your personal philosophy of what constitutes an effective leader.
* Keep a journal of your experiences during an outdoor adventure. What leadership styles did you see in the field?
* Research Shackleton and his expedition. What did you learn that was not covered in the movie?

Failure to Launch

DIRECTOR: Tom Dey

STARRING: Matthew McConaughey, Sarah Jessica Parker, Kathy Bates, Terry Bradshaw

YEAR: 2006

RATING: PG-13 (sexual content, partial nudity, and language)

RUNNING TIME: 97 min.

CORE CONCEPTS: Activity, life stages, outdoor recreation, leisure behavior

This movie is about a father and mother hiring an intervention specialist, Paula (Sarah Jessica Parker), to lure Tripp (Matthew McConaughey), their 35-year-old son, out of their house. The movie depicts Tripp's relationships with his friends and his parents. The movie is a comedy about relationships, love, and children who never leave home.

SCENES

This movie should not be shown in its entirety because many scenes do not depict recreation- or leisure-related topics. However, several scenes can be very useful for educational purposes. One scene shows Paula meeting the "boys"—Tripp and his friends—for a game of paintball. The scene depicts gender stereotypes. A few outdoor scenes can be used to show lack of judgment in the wilderness. In one scene the "boys" are mountain biking and encounter a chipmunk with comical results. Another scene shows the importance of belaying correctly when rock climbing. In the scene in which Tripp is trying to sell a boat, he explains that owning a boat is not just an activity, but also a lifestyle. This scene shows the extent to which people identify with the type of recreation they participate in.

FRAMING

Provide readings on outdoor recreation and risk management, gender roles in recreation, or leisure behavior. Ask questions such as the following:

* How do gender stereotypes affect people's recreation choices?
* How do Leave No Trace principles, judgment, and decision making affect individuals participating in outdoor recreation?
* Why do people derive an identity from their recreational interests?

DEBRIEFING QUESTIONS

Depending on the scenes selected and the course, ask questions such as the following:

* What stereotypes did Paula face when she participated in paintball?
* What risk management issues were illustrated in the two outdoor scenes? How did judgment affect what happened in these two scenes?
* What sports or recreational pursuits do you identify with personally?

CONCEPT EXPLORATION

The following activities, assignments, or discussion ideas facilitate concepts from this movie:

* Research gender roles. What activities are still associated with certain genders? Then participate in an activity that does not "fit" your gender. Reflect on this experience.
* Interview several people who identify personally with a sport or recreational activity. Find out why they enjoy that activity. In what ways are they similar to and different from each other?

Fever Pitch

DIRECTORS: Peter Farrelly, Bobby Farrelly

STARRING: Drew Barrymore, Jimmy Fallon

YEAR: 2005

RATING: PG-13 (crude and sexual humor, and some sensuality)

RUNNING TIME: 103 min.

CORE CONCEPTS: Leisure behavior, sport

B en Wrightman (Jimmy Fallon) is a high school math teacher who meets Lindsey Meeks (Drew Barrymore), a corporate workaholic, when he brings his students to her office for a field trip. He asks her out, and their relationship develops over time. He is obsessed with the Red Sox and must learn to balance the love he has for the team with the rest of his life. Their relationship is tested by his obsession.

═ SCENES ═

At least five scenes can be used to illustrate a fan's dedication to a sport team. In one, Ben and Lindsey are in the park and admit that they like each other. He tells her he is a Red Sox baseball fanatic. She invites him to meet her family at an important get-together, and he tells her about going to Florida for spring training with the Red Sox. Later in the movie, Lindsey is at home with her father. They are watching TV and see Ben interviewed in a story on the Red Sox spring training. He says that the most important things in his life, in order, are "the Red Sox, sex, and then breathing."

In another scene, Ben and Lindsey are having dinner with Lindsey's parents for the first time. Ben overhears a group at a nearby table talking about the Red Sox game, so Lindsey blocks his ears. The next day, Ben has arranged a golf time for Lindsey's parents and is spending time with them (illustrating the importance of understanding that people love different sports). In another scene Lindsey calls Ben from Paris to tell him that she is not pregnant. He pulls out a baby Red Sox outfit that he has purchased and is sad. He then picks her up from the airport. She says she loves him, but he says he still loves the Red Sox more. He is then talking to a child at a youth baseball game and the boy points out that he can love the Red Sox, but they will never love him back.

FRAMING

Provide readings on leisure behavior related to sports. Ask questions such as the following:

* Why would someone become obsessed with a sport or a sport team?
* Have you ever been obsessed with something? How can obsessions influence and change a person's life?
* What do fans do for professional sports?

DEBRIEFING QUESTIONS

This movie, or selected scenes from the movie, lend themselves to a discussion of sport as a religion. Debriefing questions may include the following:

* How do sports influence people's lives?
* Why do recreation, parks, and tourism professionals need to understand sport addictions?
* What would professional sports be without fans? Is sport mania healthy (i.e., positive) or unhealthy (i.e., negative)?

CONCEPT EXPLORATION

The following activities, assignments, or discussion ideas facilitate concepts from this movie:

* Interview fans of various sport teams. Compare their motivations for, and views of, being fans. Reflect on an experience in which you were obsessed with something. What areas of your life were affected? How did it affect people in your life?
* In what way does this movie address the concept of a sport identity? What research has been conducted on sport identity? What do people do to demonstrate a sport identity?

For Love of the Game

DIRECTOR: Sam Raimi

STARRING: Kevin Costner, Kelly Preston, John C. Reilly, Jena Malone, Brian Cox

YEAR: 1999

RATING: PG-13 (brief strong language and some sexuality)

RUNNING TIME: 137 min.

CORE CONCEPTS: Sport, activity, life stages

This movie is about a Detroit Tigers pitcher, Billy Chapel (Kevin Costner), who is near the end of his career. His team has just been sold, and the movie is a recap of the last five years of his life and how he has balanced life, love, and baseball. He must choose between being traded to another team or retiring from the game he loves. Billy has to overcome obstacles of age and physical limitations.

SCENES

This movie does a good job of developing the love story between Billy and Jane (Kelly Preston) and between Billy and baseball. At the beginning of the movie, the current owner of the Detroit Tigers comes to visit Billy and explains that he is selling the team and that Billy must decide whether he wants to be traded.

FRAMING

Provide readings on professional sports. Questions can include the following:

* What is an appropriate age at which to retire from various professional sports?
* What challenges would you face if you became physically injured and could not participate in a game or recreational activity you loved?

DEBRIEFING QUESTIONS

This movie lends itself to a discussion on sports, baseball, and life stages. Ask questions such as the following:

* What challenges did Billy overcome in his life? What role did age play?
* In what way did being a pitcher affect Billy's life?

CONCEPT EXPLORATION

The following activities, assignments, or discussion ideas facilitate concepts from this movie:

* Research the management of professional sports and learn why they sell their teams, trade players, and struggle with finances.
* Research age as a factor in playing professional sports. How does age affect different sports?

···NOW PLAYING···

Four Minutes

DIRECTOR: Charles Beeson

STARRING: Christopher Plummer, Jamie Maclachlan, Amy Rutherford, Shaun Smyth, Leon Pownall, Grahame Wood

YEAR: 2005

RATING: NR (not rated)

RUNNING TIME: 90 min.

CORE CONCEPTS: Sport, competition, teamwork, physical and mental challenge, activity, history

This movie is based on the true story of Roger Bannister, the first person to run a mile in under four minutes in 1954. The movie is about his life in the early 1950s in England, his training for the run, his life as a student of medicine, and his relationships. Other parts of history are also covered in this movie, such as the first summit of Everest by Sir Edmund Hillary.

SCENES

This movie can be shown in its entirety. If time is limited, the last race scene, in which Roger breaks the four-minute mile, is a great demonstration of the teamwork and training that went into setting this world record.

FRAMING

Provide readings on sport history, world records, or teamwork in relationship to sporting events. Ask questions such as the following:

* Which sports use teamwork?
* What world records are you aware of? Why do you think you are aware of these particular records?

DEBRIEFING

This movie lends itself to discussions on sports, competition, and teamwork. Ask questions such as the following:

* What role did teamwork play in this movie?
* What obstacles did Roger overcome in facing his challenge?
* What challenges have you almost backed away from in your life?

CONCEPT EXPLORATION

The following activities, assignments, or discussion ideas facilitate concepts from this movie:

* Learn about historical events, such as the world records covered in this movie. Talk to people who were alive during that era and ask them what they remember.
* Research world records that people are currently trying to break.

Friday Night Lights

DIRECTOR: Peter Berg

STARRING: Billy Bob Thornton, Derek Luke, Jay Hernandez, Lucas Black, Garrett Hedlund, Tim McGraw

YEAR: 2004

RATING: PG-13 (thematic issues, sexual content, language, some teen drinking, and rough sports action)

RUNNING TIME: 118 min.

CORE CONCEPTS: Sport, coaching, diversity, teamwork, family issues

This movie is based on the true story of a Texas town and its high school football team in 1988. In the town of Odessa, everyone believes in football. Amid economic and racial tensions, the team members struggle with their own personal challenges and the need to win the state championship. A lot of pressure is put on these high school students by the town, their families, and the coach to perform well on the field. They are given the opportunity to go to the state playoffs in the Texas Astrodome.

═ SCENES ═

This movie can be shown in its entirety; if time is limited, show two specific scenes. In one scene the boys are out shooting clay birds and talking about the pressure they feel; they say they don't feel as though they are only 17 years old. In another scene at a practice in the football stadium, Mike, the quarterback, is interviewed about how he believes things are going and the pressure he is under.

═ FRAMING ═

Provide readings on coaching, high school sports, or the pressure to perform in sports. Ask questions such as the following:

* ★ What challenges do high school athletes face in their sports?
* ★ What sort of pressure can a town or family put on an athlete?

DEBRIEFING QUESTIONS

This movie lends itself to a discussion on coaching, teamwork, and family issues. Ask questions such as the following:

* ★ What type of pressure did you see in the movie? Give examples.
* ★ What style of coaching was used throughout the movie? How does this style compare to other coaching styles?
* ★ What role did diversity play in this movie?

CONCEPT EXPLORATION

The following activities, assignments, or discussion ideas facilitate concepts from this movie:

* ★ The introductions of textbooks on sport often address the issue of sport as a religion. Does this movie address this concept? Have you ever known anyone for whom sport was like a religion?
* ★ Compare the coaching style in this movie to other coaching styles. Observe the coaching in a youth, high school, college, and professional game. What do you notice? How do the coaching styles vary?

··· NOW PLAYING ···

A Gentleman's Game

DIRECTOR: J. Mills Goodloe

STARRING: Mason Gamble, Dylan Baker, Philip Baker Hall, Gary Sinise, Henry Simmons, Ellen Muth

YEAR: 2001

RATING: R (language)

RUNNING TIME: 112 min.

CORE CONCEPTS: Sport, activity, coaching

Twelve-year-old Timmy Price (Mason Gamble) shows promise to become a natural and great golfer. He becomes a caddy at the local country club and learns the difference between the working class and the upper class. Timmy is mentored by former golf champion Foster Pearse (Gary Sinise), and through this relationship he learns more than just the game of golf. He also learns about life.

SCENES

This movie can be shown in its entirety. If time is limited, there is a great scene in which Timmy confronts Foster Pearse and discovers the truth about his mentor's past. In this scene Pearse talks about why he quit golf, how he played for others and not for himself, and cheating in the last tournament in which he played.

FRAMING

Provide readings on golf, class distinctions within sports, or the problems that can occur in sports. Ask questions such as the following:

* Have you ever participated in a sport for the sake of others?
* Have you ever felt that you were a natural in a sport or activity?
* What activities do you participate in that your family also participates in?

DEBRIEFING QUESTIONS

This movie lends itself to a discussion on sports and golf, coaching, and class structure. Ask questions such as the following:

* What challenges did Timmy face to learn golf?
* How did the relationship between Timmy and his father change throughout the movie?
* How does economic class affect sports and recreation?
* What relationship did Timmy have with his coach?

CONCEPT EXPLORATION

The following activities, assignments, or discussion ideas facilitate concepts from this movie:

* Interview a person who is a caddy for a living. Find out his or her background, education, and motivation for being a caddy. How

did he or she start in the profession, and is he or she able to make a living?

★ What role does family play in our leisure and recreational activities? Interview various members of your family and learn about their motivations for participating in various recreation and leisure activities.

Gladiator

DIRECTOR: Ridley Scott

STARRING: Russell Crowe, Joaquin Phoenix, Connie Nielsen, Oliver Reed, Derek Jacobi, Djimon Hounsou, Richard Harris

YEAR: 2000

RATING: R (intense, graphic combat)

RUNNING TIME: 155 min.

CORE CONCEPT: History

In AD 180, half the world's population lived under the Roman Empire. Maximus (Russell Crowe) is a general who is honored by his men and the emperor of Rome. The emperor's son kills his father and takes over as emperor, even though his father wanted Rome to be ruled by the senate. Maximus' family and home are destroyed, and he is imprisoned by the new emperor. He must fight as a gladiator to stay alive and lives only for revenge and to honor the former emperor's dying wishes.

SCENES

This movie can be shown in its entirety. Scenes that show recreational activity include the gladiator scenes, in which the audience enjoys watching men kill each other. In another scene that illustrates recreation, the gladiators play a gambling game that involves a cobra. The movie has plenty of blood and violence, and it is a good idea to let students know in advance, because some may be sensitive to gory material.

FRAMING

Provide some readings on the history of recreation, parks, and tourism. Focus specifically on the Roman era. Ask questions such as the following:

* What sort of spectator recreational activities do we currently enjoy?
* How do you think recreation varied for people from different classes during the Roman era?

DEBRIEFING QUESTIONS

This movie lends itself to a discussion on the history of the recreation, parks, and tourism movement. Ask questions such as the following:

* What did you see in this movie related to recreation? How has recreation changed since the Roman era?
* Are there any similarities between the leisure activities and sports shown in the movie and those in today's society?

CONCEPT EXPLORATION

The following activities, assignments, or discussion ideas facilitate concepts from this movie:

* Research other eras in history and compare their spectator recreational activities.
* Go to a sports arena and be a spectator. How has this experience changed since AD 180?
* Watch other movies that show sports in a particular era, and then research that era and find out how accurately the movie portrays the time period.
* Research the Roman era and the gladiators. Why did they fight? What motivates people to fight today? Why do some spectators enjoy watching fighting?

Glory Road

DIRECTOR: James Gartner

STARRING: Josh Lucas, Derek Luke, Austin Nichols, Jon Voight, Evan Jones, Schin A.S. Kerr, Alphonso McAuley, Mehcad Brooks, Sam Jones III, Damaine Radcliffe, Emily Deschanel

YEAR: 2006

RATING: PG (brief language and racial issues, including violence and epithets)

RUNNING TIME: 118 min.

CORE CONCEPTS: Sport, history, diversity, coaching, competition, teamwork

This movie is based on the true story of the 1966 Texas Western Miners coached by Don Haskins (Josh Lucas). Haskins' desire to win leads him to recruit black basketball players, which is not fully accepted at an all-white school in Texas. The movie shows the triumphs and challenges that the team faces as they compete throughout the season and make it to the NCAA championships. The movie depicts the history of racial issues that occurred during the mid-1960s.

═ SCENES ═

This movie can be shown in its entirety, or several scenes can be shown. The first part of the movie focuses on Haskins' recruitment of black students. He struggles to get the school's acceptance, the black players' acceptance, and of course, the white players' acceptance. During the credits at the end of the movie, the real players of the 1966 game talk about how it was during that time and what it was like to play basketball. These five minutes of the movie would be a great basis for a discussion.

═ FRAMING ═

Provide readings on the history of racial issues in the United States, the history of basketball, or race and sports. Ask questions such as the following:

* What do you know about people of different races playing various sports?
* What role do coaches play when leadership is needed in sports?

DEBRIEFING QUESTIONS

This movie lends itself to a discussion of sports, diversity, coaching, and teamwork. Ask questions such as the following:

* What style of coaching was used in this movie?
* What racial issues and challenges did the players face?
* Would you have done what the coach in the movie did?
* How have things changed since 1966? What struggles do teams currently face?

CONCEPT EXPLORATION

The following activities, assignments, or discussion ideas facilitate concepts from this movie:

* Interview coaches from various local junior high schools and high schools to find out what they think of racial problems within their schools and in regard to sport.
* Read articles related to issues such as race and ethnicity in regard to sports. Write a report comparing these articles to the movie.
* Have a speaker talk to your class about race or the role of race in the history of sports.

The Gods Must Be Crazy

DIRECTOR: Jamie Uys

STARRING: Marius Weyers, Sandra Prinsloo, N!xau (G/qa'o), Michael Thys

YEAR: 1980

RATING: PG (thematic elements)

RUNNING TIME: 109 min.

CORE CONCEPTS: Tourism and travel, diversity

The movie begins with a documentary-style description of the life of a Kalahari bushman named Xi (N!xau) and his family. The bushmen believe that the gods provide them only with things that are good and useful. One day, a pilot tosses an empty Coke bottle from his plane, and the bushmen find it. The bottle causes many problems among the villagers, so Xi sets off to throw it off the end of the world. The movie follows three separate story lines, eventually bringing them all together. Xi discovers many new, strange things in the world, such as cars and people with white skin. A teacher, Kate Thompson (Sandra Prinsloo), meets a doctoral student, Andrew Steyn (Marius Weyers), and a group of rebels are on the run after attacking the cabinet members of a nearby country. Xi is definitely the star of the show, with his unusual language and naive view of the world.

═ SCENES ═

If possible, show the movie in its entirety. If time is an issue, watch from the beginning through to the scene in which the assassins attack the government offices.

On some copies of the DVD, there is a special feature titled "Journey to Nyae Nyae," produced in 2003. The documentary follows a filmmaker as he seeks to find the bushman N!xau, also known as G/qa'o, who plays Xi in the movie. The documentary, an excellent follow-up to the movie, shows the reality of modern bushman life. N!xau shares his feelings about making the movies (there was a sequel) and what he wants the world to know about his people. You may want to have students watch the movie on their own time and show the documentary "Journey to Nyae Nyae" in class.

FRAMING

Ask students about their perceptions of southern Africa. Many people in Western countries picture Africa as peopled with little men in loincloths chasing lions through the underbrush. The movie plays on this stereotype when depicting the bushmen and other tribal people.

DEBRIEFING QUESTIONS

This movie lends itself to a discussion on tourism, travel, and diversity.

* Discuss the realities of life in southern Africa. There are huge cities, sprawling tenements, and tiny villages. These places are inhabited by people with great wealth and others who are truly poor. The bushmen do not live idyllic lives. Rather, they strive for food, health, and safety each day.

CONCEPT EXPLORATION

The following activities, assignments, or discussion ideas facilitate concepts from this movie:

* Research the San people of South Africa.
* Discuss how Africa is depicted in the United States. When Angelina Jolie and Brad Pitt left for Namibia to have their baby, they brought media attention to that country. Movie stars try to raise awareness of political and social injustice in the Sudan and other African countries. There is still a stereotype that all children in Africa are starving because we are constantly bombarded with such images. Street children in some African countries play on this stereotype when they beg to Western visitors, "Please, I'm starving!"

The Greatest Game Ever Played

DIRECTOR: Bill Paxton

STARRING: Shia LaBeouf, Jonathan Higgins, Stephen Dillane, Robin Wilcock, James Paxton

YEAR: 2005

RATING: PG (brief mild language)

RUNNING TIME: 120 min.

CORE CONCEPTS: History, sport, diversity, family issues, coaching

This movie is inspired by the true story of 20-year-old Francis Ouimet defeating professional golfer Harry Vardon in the 1913 U.S. Golf Open. This movie takes place in Boston, Massachusetts, in 1890 and starts when Francis sees a golf course being built near his home. He caddies for golfers for many years and is asked to play. His father struggles with the concept of golf being a career, but his mother is supportive. Francis faces the challenges of social upbringing, parental support, and his desire to play the game of golf. He is asked to play as an amateur in the U.S. Open.

═ SCENES ═

This movie can be shown in its entirety. If time is limited, a scene that addresses social class in sport shows the professional golfer, Harry Vardon, being offered his first job in London. His family background is a major topic of the conversation.

═ FRAMING ═

Provide some readings on the history of professional sports, the history of golf, or the involvement of amateurs in professional sports. Ask questions such as the following:

* ★ What do you know about the history of professional sports?
* ★ What do you know about professional golf specifically?

DEBRIEFING QUESTIONS

This movie lends itself to a discussion on history, diversity, golf, and coaching. Ask questions such as the following:

- ★ What era of U.S. history is depicted in this movie?
- ★ How have professional sports changed since this era?
- ★ What is the relationship between class status and professional sports? Does golf differ from other sports in this regard? What other sports are similar?

CONCEPT EXPLORATION

The following activities, assignments, or discussion ideas facilitate concepts from this movie:

- ★ Apply information about the history of golf to the contents of this movie.
- ★ Interview people who grew up during the Depression. Ask them about their recreation and leisure interests during that period.
- ★ Write a report comparing amateur and professional athletes.
- ★ Watch other movies that look at this era in history and compare them. Also compare other movies about golf with this movie.

· · · NOW PLAYING · · ·

Hook

DIRECTOR: Steven Spielberg

STARRING: Dustin Hoffman, Robin Williams, Julia Roberts, Bob Hoskins

YEAR: 1991

RATING: PG (some thematic elements)

RUNNING TIME: 144 min.

CORE CONCEPTS: Life stages, leisure behavior

Peter Banning (Robin Williams) is a successful lawyer, husband, and father who has trouble balancing his work and family life. Banning takes a business call during his daughter's play and sends a colleague to videotape his son's baseball game.

Peter, his wife Moira, and his children head to England for a visit with Granny Wendy. Wendy, who claims to be the "real" Wendy from the Peter Pan stories, is Moira's mother and the woman who took in a young, orphaned Peter. While in England, the Banning children are kidnapped by Captain Hook (Dustin Hoffman) and taken to Neverland. Peter meets up with Tinkerbell (Julia Roberts), who takes him back to Neverland. Once there, the Lost Boys find that the grown-up Peter has forgotten how to have fun and use his imagination. In the end, Peter Banning remembers he is really Peter Pan and fights Hook to rescue his children.

SCENES

The movie can be shown in its entirety. If time is an issue, begin with the first few minutes of the movie, from the children's play to the family's arrival at Granny Wendy's house.

Another scene takes place soon after the family arrives in London. Moira admonishes Peter for neglecting the family. She tells Peter that there are only a few years when the children really want their parents around. In the scene titled "Oh There You Are," one of the Lost Boys touches Peter's face and tries to find the child within him. The scene ends with Tinkerbell encouraging the boys to give Peter a chance to prove himself. In the scene "Feast for the Imagination," Rufio goads Peter into a massive food fight, and Peter regains his imagination and his sense of play.

FRAMING

Provide a worksheet for students to use during the viewing. Have them make notes on what childhood means to Peter, Wendy, the Lost Boys, and the other characters. Ask questions such as the following:

* How often do you play?
* What does *play* mean to you?
* What do you do for fun or play?

DEBRIEFING QUESTIONS

Develop a worksheet for students to use for reflection. Consider questions such as the following:

Teaching With Movies

* What activities do you participate in that remind you of your childhood?
* How were the characters in this movie affected by their childhoods?
* Develop analogies between the movie and real life and between childhood and the perception of freedom in adulthood.

CONCEPT EXPLORATION

The following activities, assignments, or discussion ideas facilitate concepts from this movie:

* Go outside to play a game of tag. When was the last time you played the way you did when you were a child?
* Watch young children playing. What do you notice about their interactions during play?
* Relate Peter's ability to fly to the concept of "flow," the theory developed by Mihaly Csikszentmihalyi that explains the intrinsic satisfaction that can accompany mastery of a skill.

··· NOW PLAYING ···

Hoot

DIRECTOR: Wil Shriner

STARRING: Logan Lerman, Brie Larson, Cody Linley, Brandon Agan, Luke Wilson, Tim Blake Nelson

YEAR: 2006

RATING: PG (mild bullying and brief language)

RUNNING TIME: 91 min.

CORE CONCEPTS: Leadership, environmental issues

Roy Eberhardt (Logan Lerman) is a boy who moves from Montana to Florida with his family and must settle in to a new school and make new friends. He is treated badly by the class bully and befriends two other teenagers who have a mission: to stop a construction project from destroying the home of some endangered owls.

SCENES

Two scenes illustrate the issue of environmentalism and making a difference. In one, Roy is walking with his father on the beach and explaining about the owls. He says that someone needs to stand up for what is right. His father says that he is not using good judgment. In another scene, the three kids are in a boat brainstorming about what they can do to stop the construction.

FRAMING

Provide readings on environmental issues. Ask questions such as the following:

* Have you ever taken a stand on an issue you believe in?
* What environmental issues affect you? What changes could you make regarding these issues?

DEBRIEFING QUESTIONS

This movie lends itself to a discussion on leadership, the environment, and what someone can do to make a difference. Ask questions such as the following:

* What steps did the kids in the movie take to make a difference? What steps would you recommend to make a difference in a situation like the one in the movie?
* How have you made a difference regarding an issue you believe in?

CONCEPT EXPLORATION

The following activities, assignments, or discussion ideas facilitate concepts from this movie:

* Research local environmental issues and come up with some ideas about what can be done to resolve them. Examine both sides of the situation. Interview people involved in the issue and read reports.
* As a group, choose an issue that you believe in and create a service project that will have an impact. Involve others or the media in your project.

Hotel Rwanda

DIRECTOR: Terry George

STARRING: Don Cheadle, Sophie Okonedo, Nick Nolte

YEAR: 2004

RATING: PG-13 (violence, disturbing images, and brief strong language)

RUNNING TIME: 121 min.

CORE CONCEPTS: Tourism and travel, leadership, history

Paul Rusesabagina was a very good hotel manager. In 1994, his management skills and strong ethics allowed him to save the lives of his family and over a thousand other people by opening the doors of the Hotel Des Milles Collines in Kigali to people seeking refuge from the atrocious genocide of the Hutu/Tutsi conflict. Rusesabagina kept his wits about him as he led the employees of the hotel through their regular paces, even as the Hutus massacred hundreds of thousands of Tutsis outside the gates of the hotel. Rusesabagina knew how to call in favors, bribe military officials with Scotch, and attempt to "shame" the outside world into helping. *Hotel Rwanda* is the true story of a man who stood up for himself, his family, his people, and his hotel.

SCENES

This entire movie should be shown in order for viewers to follow the storyline.

FRAMING

Provide the students with readings on the Hutu/Tutsi conflict in Rwanda. Explain the concept of genocide. Online resources include:

★ The Online NewsHour (www.pbs.org/newshour): Type "hutu" into the search frame for a number of articles.

★ Genocide.org (www.genocide.org): Select Rwanda for a link to the Human Rights Watch Web site; explore the other links for examples of global genocide.

Give each student a worksheet to assist them in viewing the movie. Include questions such as:

* What lines, or parts of the movie, were most surprising to you?
* What is the difference between Tutsis and Hutus? Are the differences real or artificial?
* What would you do if you had to leave while others stayed behind?
* How did the hotel save so many people? As was pointed out in the movie, it was a four-star hotel, not a refugee camp, and that was the image Paul Rusesabagina attempted to maintain. It was the reputation of the hotel that protected those seeking shelter.
* As the photographer boards the evacuation bus, he pushes away a man holding an umbrella for him and says, "I'm so ashamed." What does he mean by this?

DEBRIEFING QUESTIONS

Begin by reviewing the questions on the worksheet and discussing the students' responses. Ask deeper questions, such as:

* Who was right in the conflict? Support your opinion.
* Could this ever happen again?
* Are Americans truly apathetic to human atrocities around the world? Do we feel differently if it happens in Africa?
* Should countries apologize for not doing more?

CONCEPT EXPLORATION

Ask students how the genocide should be remembered or memorialized.

* Introduce them to some of the current ways the genocide is remembered. For instance, Murambi School, the site of a gruesome, planned mass execution of Tutsis, is now a memorial, complete with lime-coated bodies preserved to educate tourists. Visit http://hotzone.yahoo.com/b/hotzone/blogs1180 for more information.
* Visit www.dark-tourism.org.uk to learn about genocide memorials and the tourism that develops around them.
* If your students want to delve deeper into the Rwandan genocide, recommend books such as *Machete Season: The Killers in Rwanda Speak* by Jean Hatzfeld and *Shake Hands With the Devil: The Failure of Humanity in Rwanda*, which was written by Roméo Dallaire, the man who inspired Nick Nolte's character in the movie.

The Hudsucker Proxy

DIRECTOR: Joel Coen

STARRING: Tim Robbins, Paul Newman, Jennifer Jason Leigh, Bill Cobbs, John Mahoney

YEAR: 1994

RATING: PG (mild language)

RUNNING TIME: 111 min.

CORE CONCEPT: Commercial recreation

Norville Barnes (Tim Robbins) is a recent business school graduate from Muncie, Indiana. He travels to the city to find a career and ends up in the mailroom of Hudsucker Industries. Norville's dream is to develop a toy for children, a circular hoop that is spun around the waist (the hula hoop). Norville is promoted by Mr. Mussburger (Paul Newman), who is looking for a proxy and a patsy to lead Hudsucker Industries into the ground. Norville finally has the opportunity to develop his invention, which turns out to be a success, thereby shattering Mussburger's plans.

═ SCENES ═

Start with the scene in which Norville presents his bright idea—the hula hoop—to the Hudsucker board of directors. Show through to the scene in which Norville faces the media and begins to realize that his popularity as the CEO is waning.

═ FRAMING ═

In the movie, the lead character carries a hand-drawn picture of his great invention. Draw a circle on a piece of paper, fold the paper into a small square, and hide it in your pocket or shoe. Tell the students you have a bright idea and want to share it with them. Act very excited! Pull the paper out, rapidly unfold it, and hold it up so everyone can see the circle. Then use the line from the movie, "You know—for kids!" Tell them that it is a hula hoop, an invention central to the movie. Explain that the movie scene shows an inventor's passion for innovation. Before showing any scenes from this movie, explain the basic premise to the students.

DEBRIEFING QUESTIONS

Take the same drawing you created for the framing and tuck it back away on your person. Tell the students you have another bright idea and hold up the paper with the circle again. Norville does this in the movie, at the very end, when he announces that he has another great idea, "You know—for kids!" Ask the students what invention they think the drawing depicts (it's a Frisbee).

CONCEPT EXPLORATION

The Hudsucker Proxy is a valuable tool for facilitating a discussion of innovation. The following activities, assignments, or discussion ideas facilitate concepts from this movie:

* ★ Check the local paper for stories about inventors in your area. Invite one of them to class and ask how he or she came up with the idea for the invention. What are common characteristics of innovative people?

* ★ Use Peter Drucker's book *Innovation and Entrepreneurship* (1985) as supportive reading to continue discussions on innovation.

··· NOW PLAYING ···

The Hurricane

DIRECTOR: Norman Jewison

STARRING: Denzel Washington, John Hannah, Deborah Kara Unger, Liev Schreiber, Vicellous Reon Shannon, Dan Hedaya

YEAR: 1999

RATING: R (language and some violence)

RUNNING TIME: 145 min.

CORE CONCEPTS: Sport, activity, history, family issues

This movie is based on the true story of Rubin "Hurricane" Carter (Denzel Washington). Rubin grew up in a rough neighborhood and was a troubled youth. He became a top contender for the middle-weight boxing championship title, but was convicted of a multiple murder before he had time to compete. An African-American boy, Lesra Martin (Vicellous Reon Shannon), who lived in Canada, read his autobiography in which he claimed he was innocent and believed in him. The boy and his guardians (John Hannah, Deborah Kara Unger, and Liev Schreiber) were able to prove Rubin's innocence and get him out of jail.

SCENES

This movie can be shown in its entirety. Justice, rather than recreation, is the central theme of this movie. Several scenes in which Rubin is fighting or training to become a fighter can add to a discussion on sports or history.

FRAMING

Provide readings on African-Americans in sports and particularly in boxing. Ask questions such as the following:

* How has injustice affected sports throughout history? How has it affected sports on a personal, national, or even international level?
* What challenges do people of various backgrounds face in sport participation?

DEBRIEFING QUESTIONS

This movie lends itself to a discussion of sports and justice. Ask questions such as the following:

* How did Rubin use boxing in his life?
* What challenges or obstacles affected Rubin's boxing career?
* How can issues from this movie be applied to society today? How do justice and injustice affect sport, recreation, and leisure?

CONCEPT EXPLORATION

The following activities, assignments, or discussion ideas facilitate concepts from this movie:

* Read the book this movie is based on and analyze the life of Rubin Carter.

* Research current discrimination cases that affect people in the world today. Investigate how discrimination plays a role in leisure, recreation, and sport.
* Interview sports leaders in today's society and ask them how they feel justice affects sports.

···NOW PLAYING···

Ice Castles

DIRECTOR: Donald Wrye

STARRING: Robby Benson, Lynn-Holly Johnson, Colleen Dewhurst, Tom Skerritt, Jennifer Warren, David Huffman

YEAR: 1978

RATING: PG (adult language)

RUNNING TIME: 108 min.

CORE CONCEPTS: Recreation therapy, inclusion, competition, coaching, sport

This movie is about Alexis Winston (Lynn-Holly Johnson), a young ice skater from Iowa who has lots of natural talent and Olympic dreams. She is trained by the best. After winning a major competition, she is blinded in an accident while skating on her own. Her boyfriend, Nick Peterson (Robby Benson), encourages and supports her as she learns to skate again. The final scene shows her skating at a competition.

=== SCENES ===

This movie can be shown in its entirety even though parts of it are focused on the romance. A scene in which Alexis skates for the first time after the accident shows the challenges that she faces. Her father first brings her to a pond to skate, and then her boyfriend joins her. She is scared and unsure on the ice and needs to build confidence.

═══ FRAMING ═══

Provide some readings on people who are blinded later in life and how blindness affects them. Ask questions such as the following:

* Have you witnessed examples of inclusion in recreational activities?
* Do you think inclusion has occurred without your awareness?

═══ DEBRIEFING QUESTIONS ═══

This movie lends itself to a discussion about people with disabilities, sports, and recreation therapy. Ask questions such as the following:

* Have you faced obstacles when trying something that you strongly believe in?
* How can you include people with disabilities in recreational activities?
* What coaching styles did you see in this movie?

═══ CONCEPT EXPLORATION ═══

The following activities, assignments, or discussion ideas facilitate concepts from this movie:

* Take turns leading another person who is blindfolded and then being led while blindfolded. What challenges and obstacles did you face when you couldn't see?
* Visit people with disabilities and talk to them about how they view inclusion.
* Bring people with disabilities into class for a panel discussion.
* Participate in an activity or sport with a person with a disability.
* Interview people who coach athletes with disabilities and find out why they coach the way they do.

An Inconvenient Truth

DIRECTOR: Davis Guggenheim

DOCUMENTARY

YEAR: 2006

RATING: PG (mild thematic elements)

RUNNING TIME: 100 min.

CORE CONCEPTS: Environmental issues, leadership

In this Academy Award–winning documentary, Al Gore shares his personal lifelong commitment to the environment by looking at the issue of global warming. Gore shares personal stories, his understanding of global warming, and detailed research on the effects of global warming on the environment, including the long-term effects it will have on the earth.

SCENES

This movie should be shown in its entirety.

FRAMING

Provide some readings on environmental issues, global warming, or leadership. Ask questions such as the following:

- ★ What is global warming?
- ★ What effects do we have on the environment related to global warming?
- ★ What effect can leadership have on global warming?

DEBRIEFING QUESTIONS

This movie lends itself to a discussion on global warming and the environment. Ask questions such as the following:

- ★ How have Gore's beliefs and convictions regarding global warming affected others?

* How can each person make a difference regarding global warming?
* What are the long-term implications of global warming?
* What other effects do we have on the environment, and how will these affect others on earth in the future?

=== CONCEPT EXPLORATION ===

The following activities, assignments, or discussion ideas facilitate concepts from this movie:

* Research several environmental issues, including global warming. Read current research regarding global warming. Figure out ways that you can make a difference.
* Interview people in environmental or political leadership positions and learn about their perspectives on global warming.
* Find current newspaper and magazine articles related to the environment. Summarize the issues discussed in the articles.

··· NOW PLAYING ···

Invincible

DIRECTOR: Ericson Core

STARRING: Mark Wahlberg, Greg Kinnear, Elizabeth Banks, Kevin Conway

YEAR: 2006

RATING: PG (sports action and some mild language)

RUNNING TIME: 105 min.

CORE CONCEPTS: Coaching, leadership, sport

This movie is inspired by the true story of a part-time bartender in Philadelphia who became a professional football player for the Eagles during open tryouts. Vince Papale (Mark Wahlberg) has just lost his wife to divorce, and his life is not going well. His friends encourage him to try out for the team as a long shot. He is accepted and provides hope and inspiration for the team. Dick Vermeil (Greg Kinnear) also goes through a tough time as he is about to coach the Eagles, an underdog and a losing team.

SCENES

This movie can be shown in its entirety. If time is limited, focus on a few scenes. The first scene takes place during the open tryouts for the football team. It depicts the dedication that people have for professional teams and also the intense competition and training athletes need to go through to play professional sports. In another scene Vince has been accepted on the team, but he struggles when they are losing and goes back to his neighborhood. He watches his friends playing football in the rain and mud. They ask him to play, but he says he can't because the Eagles are playing over the weekend and he has to save himself for that game. Eventually he joins his friends and reconnects with the game of football, regaining his passion.

FRAMING

Provide readings on leadership, coaching, or Vince Papale. Ask questions such as the following:

* In what situations might underdogs succeed? What are some of the components that make a team successful?
* How can coaches and other leaders influence how people perform in professional sports?

DEBRIEFING QUESTIONS

This movie lends itself to a discussion on coaching, professional football, and leadership. Ask questions such as the following:

* How does the coaching style depicted in the movie influence Vince's performance? How does this coaching style compare to that in other movies such as *Remember the Titans* or *We Are Marshall*?
* What challenges did Vince overcome?
* How did his relationship with his team affect his performance? How did his other relationships affect his performance?

CONCEPT EXPLORATION

The following activities, assignments, or discussion ideas facilitate concepts from this movie:

* ★ Read about Vince Papale and other people who have achieved great things. Compare their motivations for success.
* ★ Compare and contrast coaching styles in various movies.

···NOW PLAYING···

K2

DIRECTOR: Franc Roddam

STARRING: Michael Beihn, Matt Craven, Raymond J. Barry, Hiroshi Fujioka, Patricia Charbonneau

YEAR: 1992

RATING: R (language)

RUNNING TIME: 102 min.

CORE CONCEPTS: Outdoor recreation, teamwork, leadership, leisure behavior, physical and mental challenge

Harold "H" Jameson (Matt Craven) and Taylor Brooks (Michael Beihn) are friends who enjoy climbing and outdoor expeditions. Harold is a professor who is torn between his wife and child and the need for the adventure of climbing. In the beginning of the movie the two are training for an ascent up McKinley in Alaska when they meet a group going to K2. H and Taylor save part of the group during an avalanche, and Taylor talks his way onto the K2 expedition. H struggles with his commitment to his family and his desire to climb the mountain. The ascent up K2 becomes a tragedy but also a success. This movie is dedicated to the first Americans to climb K2 in 1978.

SCENES

This movie can be shown in its entirety, but keep in mind that it is rated R for language. A good scene to show is the one in which the expedition is partway up K2 and the porters want to leave. Taylor burns their money to keep them going. Later in the movie, some of the porters leave, and the expedition is left with only a few porters. This scene illustrates the customs and culture of the people of Pakistan and how climbing expeditions affect the people who live in the region.

FRAMING

Provide some readings on outdoor expeditions. Questions can include the following:

* What does it take to be a successful expedition team?
* What sort of leadership is needed to make an expedition team work successfully?
* What sorts of cultures do outdoor adventurers encounter in foreign countries?

DEBRIEFING QUESTIONS

This movie lends itself to discussions on expeditions, leadership, teamwork, and communication. Questions can include the following:

* What sort of leadership was shown in the movie?
* How did this team work together to make it to the top of the mountain?
* What is needed to carry out an expedition?

CONCEPT EXPLORATION

The following activities, assignments, or discussion ideas facilitate concepts from this movie:

* After watching the movie, read a book about an outdoor expedition, such as *Touching the Void* by Joe Simpson, *Into Thin Air* by John Krakauer, *The White Spider* by Heinrich Harrer, or *Between a Rock and a Hard Place* by Aron Ralston. What kind of leadership is needed to make an expedition work? What characteristics does a person need to be part of an expedition team?
* Interview people who have participated in expeditions and ask them about their planning, leadership, and teamwork experiences.
* Watch other movies that show wilderness expeditions (for example, *Touching the Void*, *Into Thin Air*, and *The Endurance: Shackleton's Legendary Antarctic Expediton*) and compare them to this movie.

Keep Your Eyes Open

DIRECTOR: Tamra Davis

DOCUMENTARY

YEAR: 2002

RATING: PG-13 (dangerous sports action, some violence, language and drug references)

RUNNING TIME: 77 min.

CORE CONCEPTS: Activity, leisure behavior, physical and mental challenge, sport

*K*eep Your Eyes Open documents athletes in several high-risk sports, namely surfing, snowboarding, skiing, motocross (motorcycle), and freestyle BMX (cycling). The viewer gains a number of insights through interviews with the athletes, such as how activities in childhood affected the athletes' pursuit of adrenaline and what role fear plays in their pursuits.

Two professional snowboarders profiled are brother and sister. They talk about how they follow the snow around the world. When they try really dangerous stunts they "don't tell Mom until after" they live through it. Another athlete profiled is Mat Hoffman, a professional freestyle BMX stunt rider. In the movie, Mat talks about how he flatlined (nearly died) after a stunt, recovered, tried the jump again, and set a world record in doing so. Two athletes, surfer Sunny Garcia and snowboarder Marc Frank Montoya, talk about how involvement in their sports kept them from illegal activities that ended up consuming their friends.

SCENES

This movie can be watched in its entirety since there is great footage and interviews throughout. The only downside is the storyline of university security guards chasing down, and eventually running over, two skateboarders. This can, however, be incorporated into classroom discussion about skateboarding on public and private properties.

=== FRAMING ===

Give students a questionnaire to determine what high-risk activities they participate in, would like to try, or would never attempt. Put some unique sports on the sheet, such as extreme ironing (see "Concept Exploration") and heli-skiing, in order to pique the students' interests.

Consider other questions to pose, such as:

* How would you define "high-risk" recreation?
* Do people who bungee jump or BASE jump have a death wish?

=== DEBRIEFING QUESTIONS ===

After showing the movie, ask students for their immediate reactions to the athletes and their sports.

* Would the students like to try any of the activities after watching the movie?
* How did the athletes respond to people thinking they have a death wish?
* How important is fear to the athletes?
* What were some similarities in the way these athletes were raised? What type of parents did they have? What sort of sociodemographic background were they from?
* Is participation in extreme sports limited to people with higher disposable incomes?
* Why do the athletes take such personal risks?

=== CONCEPT EXPLORATION ===

Because this movie covers several sports, you have the opportunity to build off any of them and focus more deeply in one area. For instance, have students do the following:

* Investigate the development of snowboarding from the style and equipment of surfing and skateboarding.
* Research and report on other extreme sports, such as BASE jumping, tow-in surfing, free-diving, or even unusual activities such as extreme ironing (www.extremeironing.com).
* Look into how communities are protecting their properties from the damage created by illegal skateboarding and freestyle BMX riders. Architectural design and embellishments are being integrated into facility design to reduce the use of rails, stairs, and

other structures. Furthermore, skateboard and BMX parks are increasing in popularity, development, and use.

★ Show the 2001 documentary *Dogtown and Z-Boys,* which depicts the rise in popularity of skateboarding (specifically the culture and style of extreme boarding) that was developed in Southern California.

★ Show the 2004 documentary *Riding Giants,* which is about the history and culture of surfing.

···NOW PLAYING···

A League of Their Own

DIRECTOR: Penny Marshall

STARRING: Tom Hanks, Geena Davis, Madonna, Lori Petty, Rosie O'Donnell, Jon Lovitz

YEAR: 1992

RATING: PG (language)

RUNNING TIME: 128 min.

CORE CONCEPTS: Diversity, history, sport

The year is 1943 and the nation is at war. Because so many men are going overseas to fight, a girls baseball league is formed, the All-American Girls Professional Baseball League (1943-1954). This movie is based on the story of these women coming together in a time of war to play baseball as an opportunity to make money. This movie also examines a relationship between Dottie Hinson (Geena Davis) and her sister (Lori Petty). Jimmy Dugan (Tom Hanks) is the drunken former professional baseball player and manager who works with the team and eventually brings them to success. The movie starts in the present day and is a reflection of the main character, Dottie.

═ SCENES ═

This movie can be shown in its entirety. If time is limited, show the wonderful 10-minute scene in which the women enter the baseball field for the first time to try out for the AAGPBL. Throughout this scene, the movie shows news reports on what is going on in 1943 and why the baseball league is being formed. Players are chosen for the four teams, and the women are told they will play in dresses and must attend finishing school. The scene at the finishing school reveals the intention to sell women's baseball based on the players' looks.

☰ FRAMING ☰

Provide reading on women and recreation, the history of women in sports, or gender equity issues. Ask questions such as the following:

* How has history shaped women's roles in recreation and sports?
* What value does the United States place on professional sports?
* What started women's professional baseball?

☰ DEBRIEFING QUESTIONS ☰

This movie lends itself to a discussion of history of women's baseball and diversity. Ask questions such as the following:

* How does the role of women in professional sports today compare to that in 1943?
* How did the AAGPBL influence other professional sports?
* What roles have uniforms and sexuality played in sports?

☰ CONCEPT EXPLORATION ☰

The following activities, assignments, or discussion ideas facilitate concepts from this movie:

* Of the professional sport leagues that exist currently, which are men's teams and which are women's teams?
* Research the role of women in professional sports such as baseball and compare it to the role of men in similar sports.
* Compare textbooks' treatment of the issue of women in sports with this movie. Discuss Title IX and other issues related to gender and equality.
* What would have happened if men had to go to finishing school? What are the current standards for a professional athlete to be "finished," or "professional looking"? What sells, and how does it sell?

The Lorax

DIRECTOR: Hawley Pratt

STARRING: Intro by Eddie Albert and voice of Bob Holt

YEAR: 1972

RATING: G

RUNNING TIME: 30 min.

CORE CONCEPT: Environmental issues

The Lorax, a character created by Dr. Seuss, speaks for the trees. He wants things to stay the same and is against building and destroying the environment. The Once-ler discovers the value of the trees, and his greed causes the destruction of the forest. The Once-ler brings in his family, creates roads, builds houses, and establishes a city. The Lorax explains to the Once-ler several times that because of his actions, all the animals must leave. Once all the resources are gone, the Once-ler's factory stops producing and everything is gray, dirty, and dark as a result of the excess population and environmental damage.

SCENES

We recommend that you view the entire movie, which is only 30 minutes long.

FRAMING

Provide some readings on leisure and the natural environment or environmental education. Ask questions such as the following:

* What is the role of recreation in the protection of the environment?
* In what way does the use of the environment for recreation contribute to its destruction?
* What forms of recreation play the largest role in using the environment?

DEBRIEFING QUESTIONS

This movie lends itself to a discussion on the impact of recreation on the environment. Debriefing questions can include the following:

* How have you used the environment for recreation purposes?

* How does popular or mass culture recreation affect the environment?

* What is the long-term impact of using the environment for recreation purposes?

CONCEPT EXPLORATION

The following activities, assignments, or discussion ideas facilitate concepts from this movie:

* Keep track of how many times you use the natural environment for recreation purposes over the course of a month. How did you use it? What impact did you have? What impact did you see from other users?

* Bring in newspaper articles on the environment. How do the issues discussed in the articles relate to the recreation, parks, and tourism field?

* Interview city and regional planners, corporate executives, and land users about their views on leisure and the natural environment. Then write a paper on what you learn.

* How does sustainable development relate to this movie?

Mad Hot Ballroom

DIRECTOR: Marilyn Agrelo

DOCUMENTARY

YEAR: 2005

RATING: PG (some thematic elements)

RUNNING TIME: 105 min.

CORE CONCEPTS: Activity, teamwork, coaching, leisure behavior, diversity, competition

This documentary is about the 10-week ballroom dance program that was added to the New York City public school curriculum for fifth-graders in 1994. In 2005 over 6,000 children from 60 schools were required to take the 10-week curriculum. This documentary follows the students through the curriculum, examining the skills they learn through social dance lessons, the coaching they experience, and the teamwork that develops. This movie also shows how the students and teachers deal with competition and the pride of winning or the heartbreak of losing.

═ SCENES ═

This movie can be shown in its entirety to examine leisure education. If time is limited, a few scenes illustrate the main topics of the movie. During a scene in the first part of the movie, the principal of one of the schools talks about the kids and where they come from. She discusses the importance of having the social dance curriculum and why her school chooses to support it. She explains that dance is more than physical education; it encompasses etiquette, knowledge of other cultures, and life. In another scene, Wilson, a student who doesn't understand English, demonstrates a dance he is very good at. In a scene during the final competition, a principal talks about Michelle, a student who was always getting into trouble. Her behavior has changed since she took part in the social dance curriculum.

FRAMING

Provide reading on leisure education, leisure and recreation in public schools, or competition. Ask questions such as the following:

* What sort of leisure education did you have in elementary school?
* What leisure education is currently being provided in public schools?
* What is the value of leisure education in public schools?

DEBRIEFING QUESTIONS

This movie lends itself to a discussion on dance, coaching, teamwork, and competition. Ask questions such as the following:

* What is the value of competition for these students?
* How can social dance influence other areas of their lives?
* What is the philosophy of winning in the movie? Do you agree with this philosophy?

CONCEPT EXPLORATION

The following activities, assignments, or discussion ideas facilitate concepts from this movie:

* Visit local public schools and research the types of leisure education they provide. Talk to students, principals, teachers, and parents about leisure education in their schools.
* Research social dance (either by taking a social dance class or by interviewing people who dance on a regular basis). What do people gain from social dance experiences?

The Milagro Beanfield War

DIRECTOR: Robert Redford

STARRING: Ruben Blades, Chick Vennera, Sonia Braga, Christopher Walken

YEAR: 1988

RATING: R (language)

RUNNING TIME: 117 min.

CORE CONCEPTS: Commercial recreation, tourism and travel

The small town of Milagro, New Mexico, is dying. A developer, Ladd Devine, has bought up land and is creating a recreation area outside of town. Devine needs more land for his golf course and confronts Joe Mondragon, a farmer who won't sell. Joe decides to replant his dead father's beanfield using water he has diverted from a government line. The interests of the community and the developer come to a head, with neighbors fighting and the developer and local government trying to get Joe to change his plans. This movie illustrates the impacts of development on rural communities.

SCENES

The movie can be watched in its entirety; however, three scenes can be shown to great effect. The first two scenes set the story, giving the viewer a feel for the town of Milagro and insight into why Joe allowed the water to run into the beanfield. Scene 8, "Talk of the Town," depicts a town meeting about the development and beanfield. Ruby, a local activist, and the local journalist try to explain why Devine's development will destroy the town. This scene depicts the problem of poor tourism planning from the community's perspective.

FRAMING

Have students get into small groups. Ask them to consider the pros and cons of the development of a commercial recreation area in a small, rural town in the U.S. Southwest (population 400). Give them the freedom to define what the recreation area includes and what industries may already be in the town.

DEBRIEFING QUESTIONS

After watching the movie, have students discuss the pros and cons they came up with in the framing exercise. Ask questions such as the following:

* How did your descriptions of the recreation area and the town compare to that of the movie?
* How do the events in the movie reflect planning theories and processes?
* How could the recreation area in the movie have been planned differently to better serve both the community and the developer?

CONCEPT EXPLORATION

Use this movie as an introduction to agricultural tourism. The following activities, assignments, or discussion ideas facilitate concepts from this movie:

* If agriculture is a significant industry in your area, invite some local farmers and ranchers to talk about the pros and cons of development and how it affects agricultural areas.
* Go to an agricultural tourism site and learn about agritourism as part of rural tourism development initiatives.

· · · NOW PLAYING · · ·

Million Dollar Baby

DIRECTOR: Clint Eastwood

STARRING: Clint Eastwood, Hilary Swank, Morgan Freeman, Jay Baruchel, Mike Colter

YEAR: 2004

RATING: PG-13 (violence, some disturbing images, thematic material, and language)

RUNNING TIME: 132 min.

CORE CONCEPTS: Sport, coaching, competition, diversity

This movie won four Academy Awards. It is about a 31-year-old poor waitress from a dysfunctional family who has a strong desire to box. Maggie Fitzgerald (Hilary Swank) tries to convince Frankie Dunn (Clint Eastwood) to coach her and be her manager. Frankie is estranged from his own daughter. Through the eyes of Eddie "Scrap-Iron" Dupris (Morgan Freeman), the narrator of the story, Frankie trains and accepts Maggie as a boxer and daughter. This movie focuses on the trusting and loving friendship that develops between Maggie and Frankie.

═══ SCENES ═══

Two scenes are appropriate for students. In the first, Maggie is in the gym training on her 32nd birthday. Frankie asks why she is there, and she gives all the reasons that he should train her. He listens, and they start working together. The dialogue is about how they will relate as a coach and trainee. In another scene, one of the boxers at the gym beats up Danger (a "slower" boxer) in the ring. This scene illustrates injustice, ability differences, and bullying.

═══ FRAMING ═══

Provide readings on women's boxing or coaching styles. Ask questions such as the following:

★ What impact has women's involvement in traditionally male sports had on society?

★ How has a coach influenced your life?

═══ DEBRIEFING QUESTIONS ═══

This movie lends itself to a discussion of boxing, coaching, competition, and diversity. Ask questions such as the following:

★ What challenges did Maggie overcome to become a boxer?

★ What barriers did Frankie face as he coached Maggie?

★ What role did Morgan Freeman's character play in this movie?

═══ CONCEPT EXPLORATION ═══

The following activities, assignments, or discussion ideas facilitate concepts from this movie:

★ Visit a boxing gym and interview people who box to learn their motivations for taking up the sport. Try to interview both men and women and compare their motivations.

* Research the history of women in boxing.
* Examine the coaching in this movie and compare it to coaches that you know. Also, compare the coaching style in this movie to that in other movies.

··· NOW PLAYING ···

Miracle

DIRECTOR: Gavin O'Connor

STARRING: Kurt Russell, Eddie Cahill, Patricia Clarkson, Noah Emmerich

YEAR: 2004

RATING: PG (language and some rough sports action)

RUNNING TIME: 135 min.

CORE CONCEPTS: Teamwork, sport, coaching, leadership, competition

Miracle is the true story of the 1980 U.S. ice hockey team and their challenges to work as a newly developed team. Herb Brooks (Kurt Russell) coaches and trains the "underdog team." With a demanding practice schedule and only months to train for the Olympics, the team faces challenges and at the end celebrates a victory over the Soviet Union team in Lake Placid, New York.

══ SCENES ══

The movie can be shown in its entirety. If time is limited, show the scene in which the team is practicing on the ice. The coach asks the team members to introduce themselves and state the name of the team they skate for. The players keep introducing themselves and their teams throughout the first several months of practices. After losing a "friendly" competition match with the Soviet Union, the coach makes the team continue to practice. He keeps saying "again" and "again" as the players are falling down with exhaustion. Finally, one of the team members introduces himself and says that he plays for the United States. The coach lets them stop skating and is glad to see that they are now skating for the sake of the team and not just to prove they are better than the other players. This scene can be used as a jumping-off point for a discussion of coaching strategies and the pressure to form a team from individuals who used to compete against each other.

═══ FRAMING ═══

Provide reading on coaching and sports. Ask questions such as the following:

⭑ Describe some of the challenges of forming a team with individuals who used to compete against one another.

⭑ What coaching strategies have you seen that have been successful? Not successful?

⭑ How do sports influence relationships with other people and other countries?

═══ DEBRIEFING QUESTIONS ═══

This movie lends itself to a discussion on coaching, ice hockey, the Olympics, and teamwork. Ask questions such as the following:

⭑ What would it be like to be on an Olympic team?

⭑ How can future coaches or recreation professionals prepare to work with a variety of teams?

⭑ How have the Olympics become part of our society? How does the history of the Olympics influence society today?

═══ CONCEPT EXPLORATION ═══

The following activities, assignments, or discussion ideas facilitate concepts from this movie:

⭑ Watch a variety of coaching styles and reflect on the power of a coach. Keep a journal of what you see and what works and doesn't work for various teams.

⭑ Research the history of the Olympics and the involvement of various nations in the Olympic competitions. What are some reasons countries have not participated? How do you think this might change in the future?

⭑ Watch a professional men's and a professional women's hockey or basketball game on TV. How do they differ? How are they similar?

The Motorcycle Diaries

DIRECTOR: Walter Salles

STARRING: Gael Garcia Bernal, Rodrigo de la Serna, Mia Maestro

YEAR: 2004

RATING: R (language)

RUNNING TIME: 126 min.

CORE CONCEPT: Tourism and travel

Revolutionary leader and popular culture icon Ernesto "Ché" Guevara was a promising medical student in Buenos Aires, Argentina, before he and his friend Alberto Granado (a biochemist) set off on a journey across Latin America. On the back of a temperamental motorcycle, Alberto and Ernesto encounter new cultures, poverty, political upheaval, and in the end, themselves. They complete their journey in a leper colony in the Peruvian Amazon, donating their time and experience to a community displaced by disease and the stigmas attached to it by society. In the end, the two men discover both invisible and tangible divisions between rich and poor, healthy and sick. The men who begin the journey are not the same as those who end the journey.

SCENES

The movie should be shown in its entirety. Although many scenes involve only picturesque shots of the Latin American landscape and could be passed over to save time, the landscape is as much a character in the movie as the human actors. If time limits exist, the first scenes portraying Ernesto and Alberto as young, optimistic adventurers can be compared with scenes from the middle and end of the movie, particularly their encounters with miners at the Chuquicamata Copper Mine in Chile, their time in Machu Picchu in Peru, and the time they spend in the leper colony.

FRAMING

Make sure students know that this movie is in Spanish with English subtitles.

* Provide background information on travel motivation models; those of Plog, Pearce, and Iso-Ahola may be good places to start. If students are not familiar with the terms *adventure travel* and *cultural tourism,* you may want to define them.

* Provide some background regarding Latin American culture and vocabulary from the film. Here are some examples: Maté, leprosy, Chuquicamata Copper Mine, Pablo Neruda, and Machu Picchu.

* Provide some background about Ernesto Guevara, who remains a controversial figure. Students may or may not know the role he played in Castro's revolution in Cuba, as well as other campaigns in Bolivia and the Congo. Emphasize that this movie is adapted from Guevara's own accounts of his travels in Latin America. Explaining that the period of Guevara's life presented in the film occurred before he became a revolutionary may help to avoid politically sensitive discussions.

DEBRIEFING QUESTIONS

The Motorcycle Diaries can be a source of discussion about many topics, including travel motivations, adventure travel, and cultural tourism. However, topics such as social justice, social change, and volunteerism can also be addressed. Pose questions such as, "How have your travels changed you?" and, "Why do you travel?" Other questions include the following:

* Ernesto and Alberto immerse themselves in each destination. They interact with and engage locals in conversation and learn from all of them. Would you characterize this as typical tourist behavior? Would you classify this as part of adventure travel?

* Ernesto and Alberto incorporated their interests and passions (medicine and service) into their adventure by volunteering at the leper colony. How would you incorporate your interests and passions into an adventure? Would such an experience qualify as a vacation? Why or why not?

* Consider the transformation of Alberto and Ernesto. What were they like at the beginning of the movie compared to at the end? What created the transformation?

* Using your own words and opinions, define *adventure travel.* What, for you, is *cultural tourism*? How does it enhance your understanding of a culture? What impact does this form of tourism have on the culture it is spotlighting?

* Tourism is often referred to as a "smokestackless industry" because of the misperception that it doesn't create any environmental impacts. Does the same misperception exist for the social impacts of tourism? Is tourism an equalizer of rich and poor, or is it a dividing line?

* Discuss the aspects of social justice and equity presented in the film. How were the poor or indigenous people in the film treated as opposed to the wealthier members of society?

═ CONCEPT EXPLORATION ═

The following activities, assignments, or discussion ideas facilitate concepts from this movie:

* Create a travel and recreation journal and record your own adventures—whether they take you across the country or across town. What were your motivations for your activities? Who did you go with and what did you do? Who did you meet?

* If you were to go on an adventure like that shown in *The Motorcycle Diaries,* who would you want to go with and why? Where would you go? Would your plan be one of "improvisation" like that of Ernesto and Alberto? Why or why not?

* Ernesto and Alberto donated their time in a leper colony because they had interests in medicine and because they were motivated to help people in need. Many college students are making the decision to go on "alternative spring breaks" where they perform public service. On your campus, contact the alternative spring break liaison (or similar service) and interview participants in the program. Ask them about their motivations: Were they interested in the experience, the destination, or spending time with friends? Reflect on your own feelings about such programs: Would you participate? Why or why not?

Moulin Rouge

DIRECTOR: Baz Luhrmann

STARRING: Nicole Kidman, Ewan McGregor, John Leguizamo, Jim Broadbent, Richard Roxburgh

YEAR: 2001

RATING: PG-13 (sexual content)

RUNNING TIME: 127 min.

CORE CONCEPTS: Diversity, history

This movie takes place in Paris in 1899. Christian (Ewan McGregor) is a hopeful poet who wants to live in the world of the Moulin Rouge, a world of theater, dance, drugs, and prostitution. Christian falls in love with Satine (Nicole Kidman), the star of the show and the city's famous prostitute. The love affair is played out as she struggles to keep her job. She wants to become a star and will do almost anything to achieve her goal.

SCENES

In a scene that depicts the difference between the rich and the poor, Christian goes to Moulin Rouge for the first time. Everyone is dancing, including Satine (Nicole Kidman). The scene shows the drugs, drinking, and dancing that took place during the era (even though the music is current).

FRAMING

Provide some readings on the history of recreation in Europe at the turn of the 20th century. Ask students to explain how socioeconomic class affected recreation and leisure in the past and today.

DEBRIEFING QUESTIONS

This movie lends itself to a discussion on diversity and history. Ask questions such as the following:

* What types of taboo recreation are depicted in this movie? How has this changed since 1899?

★ What role does theater currently play in society and in relation to recreation and leisure?

CONCEPT EXPLORATION

The following activities, assignments, or discussion ideas facilitate concepts from this movie:

★ Research the history of theater, specifically in Europe. How has theater changed from the era depicted in the movie to the present day?

★ Examine books and other movies related to the history of the theater and acting. What trends have occurred? In what way do theater productions today reflect those of the past?

··· NOW PLAYING ···

Mr. Miami Beach: The Remarkable Story of Carl Fisher

DIRECTOR: Mark J. Davis

DOCUMENTARY

YEAR: 1998

RATING: NR (not rated)

RUNNING TIME: 56 min.

CORE CONCEPTS: Commercial recreation, tourism and travel

Although Carl Fisher may not be someone we read about in history books, he is responsible for shaping many attractions we are familiar with today. Fisher held the first patent for automobile headlights, built the Indianapolis Speedway, was instrumental in the development of both the Lincoln Highway and the Dixie Highway, and is the creator of Miami Beach, Florida. Before Fisher and his amazing vision took over, the Miami Beach area was a wild swampland. Fisher turned it into a destination for the wealthy by rebuilding the area from the ground up. This film follows Fisher's life from his early days as a troubled schoolboy, through his glory years, to the bitter end of his amazing life.

SCENES

This film is best shown in its entirety.

FRAMING

Have students do word association, brainstorming, or mind mapping with "Miami Beach" as the starting point. Ask them how they think Miami Beach got its start.

DEBRIEFING QUESTIONS

Have students write a short reaction to the film based on their initial thoughts about the origins of Miami Beach. Collect the reflections and read a few (without naming the students). Ask questions such as the following:

* How did Miami Beach change after Carl Fisher left for Montauk?
* How has Miami Beach changed since Carl Fisher's death?

CONCEPT EXPLORATION

The following activities, assignments, or discussion ideas facilitate concepts from this movie:

* Have students listen to the Will Smith song "Miami," watch an episode of the television series *Miami Vice,* or research what movies have been filmed at Miami Beach.
* Research other vacation or resort communities and how they got their start.

Murderball

DIRECTORS: Henry Rubin, Dana Shapiro

DOCUMENTARY

YEAR: 2005

RATING: R (language and sexual content)

RUNNING TIME: 88 min.

CORE CONCEPTS: Coaching, recreation therapy, physical and mental challenge, competition, teamwork, diversity

This documentary follows the life of Mark Zupan and the U.S. Olympic wheelchair rugby team as they reach their goals and compete in the 2004 Paralympics. This movie is about human spirit and the inspiration that comes from the members of this team. The men play wheelchair rugby in armored wheelchairs and challenge teams from throughout the world. Many of the characters' stories are developed in the movie.

SCENES

This movie can be shown in its entirety. If time is limited, show the scene in which the U.S. team is competing in Athens at the Paralympics. This scene shows the true competitive nature and skill of the sport of wheelchair rugby. In another good scene the men talk about playing in the Paralympics and not the Special Olympics. If you are showing the entire movie, it would be wise to prepare students for a section of the movie in which the men explain how they maintain healthy sexual activity. If your audience is young, consider showing only the two suggested scenes.

FRAMING

Provide readings on murderball, the Paralympics, people with disabilities, or coaching styles. Ask questions such as the following:

* What sports do people in wheelchairs participate in? What challenges must they overcome?
* What stereotypes are placed on people in wheelchairs?

DEBRIEFING QUESTIONS

Debriefing can include a discussion on therapeutic recreation, coaching, people with disabilities, teamwork, or the Paralympics. Questions can include the following:

* ★ How was rugby adapted for people in wheelchairs?
* ★ How are other sports adapted?
* ★ What role has technology played in therapeutic recreation?
* ★ What coaching styles were used in this movie?
* ★ What role do people's personalities play in competitive sports?

CONCEPT EXPLORATION

The following activities, assignments, or discussion ideas facilitate concepts from this movie:

* ★ Research the Paralympics, including when it began, how sports are modified, and what sports are played. Have a person who uses a wheelchair visit your classroom. Learn his or her story and the influence technology has had on his or her life.
* ★ Research the Special Olympics and the Paralympics. What are the differences between these two organizations? Who participates in each?

· · · NOW PLAYING · · ·

My Left Foot

DIRECTOR: Jim Sheridan

STARRING: Daniel Day-Lewis, Ray McAnally, Brenda Fricker, Alison Whelan

YEAR: 1989

RATING: R (language)

RUNNING TIME: 103 min.

CORE CONCEPTS: Recreation therapy, leisure behavior, inclusion

This movie is told as a flashback of the story of Christy Brown (Daniel Day-Lewis), who was born to a poor Irish family and with crippling cerebral palsy. His mother sees hope in him and believes in him. He learns to communicate and eventually write and create art with his only working limb, his left foot.

SCENES

This movie can be shown in its entirety. In one particular scene that shows the importance of recreation to Christy Brown, he is playing soccer with his brother and the other local kids. He struggles to play but is obviously enjoying himself. Several other scenes show Christy painting, which illustrates the importance of art as a form of recreation.

FRAMING

Provide some readings on therapeutic recreation, cerebral palsy, or art as a form of recreation. Ask questions such as the following:

* What experiences have you had being around people with a disability such as cerebral palsy?
* What forms of recreation have you used as a therapeutic outlet?

DEBRIEFING QUESTIONS

This movie lends itself to a discussion on therapeutic recreation or people with cerebral palsy. Questions can include the following:

* How has therapeutic recreation changed since the mid-1900s?
* What other forms of recreation are an outlet for people with disabilities?

CONCEPT EXPLORATION

The following activities, assignments, or discussion ideas facilitate concepts from this movie:

* Research cerebral palsy and learn how it affects people.
* Visit people who have cerebral palsy and find out whether therapeutic recreation is part of their lives and how.
* Create a recreation or leisure program for people with cerebral palsy and then implement this program with a local agency.

Mystery, Alaska

DIRECTOR: Jay Roach

STARRING: Russell Crowe, Hank Azaria, Mary McCormack, Lolita Davidovich, Ron Eldard, Colm Meaney, Maury Chaykin, Burt Reynolds

YEAR: 1999

RATING: R (language and sexuality)

RUNNING TIME: 119 min.

CORE CONCEPTS: Sport, teamwork

The amateur ice hockey team of Mystery, Alaska, must come together to face the New York Rangers. In Mystery, Alaska, hockey players skate at a very early age, and the town watches the team religiously. Hockey and sports are very important to the community. The entire town unites and works together to be part of the nationally televised competition.

SCENES

This movie can be shown in its entirety, but be aware that nudity and language occur throughout the movie. If time is an issue, the beginning of the movie shows people in the town participating in several forms of winter recreation. In a scene that shows the community's pride in its hockey team, several people read the article in *Sports Illustrated* that features their hockey team. In another scene, the townspeople have a meeting to discuss whether to invite the Rangers to their town to play hockey.

FRAMING

Provide some readings on community involvement with sports, teamwork, or coaching. Ask questions such as the following:

* Have you ever been part of a community that supported one specific sport or activity?
* What are some ways communities demonstrate involvement with a sport team?
* In what way are sports rituals for some people?

DEBRIEFING QUESTIONS

This movie can be used for a discussion on ritual, community involvement with leisure, sports, or teamwork. Debriefing questions can include the following:

* How did this team come together during the course of the movie?
* How did ice hockey become a ritual for Mystery, Alaska?
* How can a sport unite a town?

CONCEPT EXPLORATION

The following activities, assignments, or discussion ideas facilitate concepts from this movie:

* Visit a community for which a given sport is a ritual. Interview people in the community.
* Research a community that revolves around a specific sport or activity. Read newspaper articles from the community related to the activity or sport.
* What sports are part of community rituals in various parts of the world? How do they affect the communities? How does this differ on the various continents?

· · · NOW PLAYING · · ·

Patch Adams

DIRECTOR: Tom Shadyac

STARRING: Robin Williams, Daniel London, Monica Potter, Philip Seymour Hoffman

YEAR: 1998

RATING: PG-13 (strong language and crude humor)

RUNNING TIME: 115 min.

CORE CONCEPTS: Recreation therapy, diversity

The movie is based very loosely on the book, *Gesundheit! Bringing Good Health to You, the Medical System, and Society Through Physician Service, Complementary Therapies, Humor, and Joy* by Patch Adams and Maureen Mylander. Hunter Adams (Robin Williams) changes the direction of his life after a short stay in a mental institution where he realizes he wants to help people by becoming a doctor. This is also where he develops his nickname, Patch. The movie chronicles his time as a student at the Medical College of Virginia during the 1960s and his constant battles with the medical establishment. During the course of his studies, he uses laughter to better the lives of patients and help chronically ill patients accept death. Patch and his fellow medical students start a free clinic that would slowly evolve into the Gesundheit Institute. However, the clinic results in the death of one of the main characters and the expulsion of Patch from medical school.

SCENES

The scenes at the mental institution illustrate stereotypes about people with mental disabilities and are quite funny. One of the most memorable scenes is with Patch and a terminal cancer patient played by Peter Coyote. This can be used to discuss attitudes toward death and quality of life issues. Several scenes contain brief male nudity.

FRAMING

Point out that the children in the movie are real patients from the Make-A-Wish Foundation, which adds a note of realism. Have students break into small groups and discuss the following:

* Can laughter cure illness?
* Is leisure a part of mental and physical health?
* How do you view death?
* How can recreation be used as therapy?
* What is your passion in life?

DEBRIEFING QUESTIONS

Explain that the movie manipulates the actual elements of Patch's life for the sake of entertainment and dramatic interest. Even though the movie is "based on a true story," it is very different from the book. Have students visit www.patchadams.org for additional information on the Gesundheit Institute. Ask questions such as the following:

* In what ways is Patch Adams' story different from the movie?
* Why do you think the dream of a free hospital was never realized?

=== **CONCEPT EXPLORATION** ===

The following activities, assignments, or discussion ideas facilitate concepts from this movie:

* Read the book *Gesundheit!* by Patch Adams in conjunction with the movie.
* Try doing goofy things in public and recording people's reactions. Were you embarrassed to be doing something outside the norm? Were reactions positive or negative?
* Plan your own funeral and write your own eulogy. Find out the actual costs of a funeral service and discuss why costs are so high.

· · · NOW PLAYING · · ·

Project Grizzly

DIRECTOR: Peter Lynch

DOCUMENTARY

YEAR: 1996

RATING: NR (not rated)

RUNNING TIME: 72 min.

CORE CONCEPTS: Outdoor recreation, leisure behavior, physical and mental challenge

A close encounter with a grizzly bear changed the life of Troy Hurtubise. He undertook a mission to build a protective suit that would allow him to safely interact with grizzly bears in the wild. The documentary follows his field testing of the Ursus Mark VI, which took seven years and $150,000 to develop. Hurtubise gets hit by a three-ton truck, beaten with baseball bats, pushed off a cliff, set on fire, and shot with a 12-gauge shotgun. The ending is slightly unsettling because his attempts to greet the "old man," as he calls the bear, are quickly derailed after he discovers he can't walk on uneven ground in the suit. The film is also interesting from a pop culture perspective because it has been spoofed on *The Simpsons* in an episode titled "The Fat and the Furriest" and lauded by director Quentin Tarantino as his favorite documentary.

SCENES

This film can be shown in its entirety. The scenes of the field testing of the Ursus Mark VI and Hurtubise's earlier attempts to build a bear-proof suit are good examples of the lengths someone will go to in pursuit of serious leisure.

FRAMING

The World Leisure Commission on Education defined serious leisure as "the systematic pursuit of deep satisfaction through an amateur, hobbyist, or volunteer activity that participants find so substantial and interesting that, in the typical case, they launch themselves on a (non-work) career centered on acquiring and expressing its special skills, knowledge, and experience" (Stebbins, 2000).

DEBRIEFING QUESTIONS

This movie lends itself to a discussion on leisure behavior, outdoor recreation, and physical and mental challenges. Ask questions such as the following:

* What are some examples of serious leisure?
* Do you engage in serious leisure?
* Discuss how the grizzly project meets the requirements of serious leisure. Is Hurtubise crazy, self-delusional, or a visionary?

CONCEPT EXPLORATION

The following activities, assignments, or discussion ideas facilitate concepts from this movie:

* Discuss the dimensions or characteristics of serious leisure and how the grizzly project compares. Discuss other examples of movies that depict serious leisure such as *Best in Show, Fever Pitch,* and *Trekkies.*

Radio

DIRECTOR: Michael Tollin

STARRING: Cuba Gooding Jr., Ed Harris, Alfre Woodard, Debra Winger

YEAR: 2003

RATING: PG (mild language and thematic elements)

RUNNING TIME: 109 min.

CORE CONCEPTS: Coaching, sport, diversity, inclusion

This movie depicts the relationship between a high school football coach (Ed Harris) and Radio (Cuba Gooding Jr.), a young man with mental retardation and a heart of gold. As the coach develops trust with him, the entire high school and community come to respect and appreciate this caring person. This movie was inspired by true events that took place in South Carolina in 1976.

═ SCENES ═

This movie can be shown in its entirety. If time is limited, the scene in which Radio first helps with the high school team shows his excitement about working with the team, as well as the interactions he has with the team members. In another scene Radio is on the field during the game and yells out loud the coach's instructions for the next play. This tips the other team off, and they gain possession of the football. Later, in the barbershop, the fathers of the players tell the coach that Radio is a distraction to the team.

═ FRAMING ═

Provide some readings on people with disabilities, coaching, or diversity. Ask questions such as the following:

* ★ Have you ever worked with people with disabilities? What did you learn?
* ★ In what ways are physical and mental disabilities similar, and in what ways are they different? What impact does sport have on each?

DEBRIEFING QUESTIONS

This movie lends itself to a discussion on inclusion, mental retardation, sports, and coaching. Ask questions such as the following:

* What inspired the coach to believe in Radio?
* How did the players learn to work with Radio?
* What challenges did Radio, the players, the coach, and the school have to overcome during the movie?

CONCEPT EXPLORATION

The following activities, assignments, or discussion ideas facilitate concepts from this movie:

* Research mental retardation and learn how it affects people.
* Visit people with mental retardation and find out whether therapeutic recreation is used in their lives and how.
* Compare the coaching style depicted in this movie to other coaching styles you have seen in real life or in other movies. How are leadership theories reflected in coaching styles?

··· NOW PLAYING ···

Remember the Titans

DIRECTOR: Boaz Yakin

STARRING: Denzel Washington, Will Patton, Wood Harris, Ryan Hurst, Ethan Suplee, Donald Faison

YEAR: 2000

RATING: PG (thematic elements and some language)

RUNNING TIME: 113 min.

CORE CONCEPTS: Diversity, teamwork, sport, leisure behavior, leadership, coaching

This film is based on a true story from 1971. Coach Herman Boone (Denzel Washington) comes into a town to coach the high school football team after the demotion of a white coach (Will Patton) to assistant coach. The two men have to learn to work together to successfully coach the football team, which is a combination of black and white students whose high schools were combined. This story examines the training and teamwork that the students must face as they learn to work together and respect each other.

SCENES

The movie can be shown in its entirety. If time is an issue, several scenes capture the essence of the story. In one 15- to 20-minute scene the football team is in the cafeteria of the summer training camp. The coach asks them to share personal information with each other, but they are unable to do this. He tells them they will have hard practices until they get to know their teammates. Hard practices continue as the team members interview each other. Later in the movie the coach wakes the team up very early one morning and they run to Gettysburg. He uses the setting to talk about how the team is still fighting over the issues Americans fought over during the Civil War. In another scene the team is showering and one player tries to kiss another. The other team members are repulsed and have to deal with their feelings about homosexuality.

FRAMING

Provide readings on leisure and race and ethnicity. Ask questions such as the following:

* What racial issues have you faced in leisure and recreation settings?
* Do you think this country has changed in recent years regarding race and ethnicity?

DEBRIEFING QUESTIONS

This movie lends itself to a discussion on teamwork, sports, leadership, and leisure behavior. Ask questions such as the following:

* Does it surprise you that the events of this movie took place in 1971? How has society changed since then? Has it changed everywhere in the United States?
* What can you do to make a difference in regard to race and ethnicity?

* How might racial issues affect you as a recreation, parks, and tourism professional?
* What role does sexuality play in sports? What effect does it have on high school, college, and professional teams?

=== **CONCEPT EXPLORATION** ===

The following activities, assignments, or discussion ideas facilitate concepts from this movie:

* Interview coaches from various local junior high schools and high schools to find out what they think of racial problems within their schools and in regard to sport in general.
* Read articles related to issues such as race and ethnicity in sports. Write a report comparing these articles to the movie.
* Have a speaker come in and talk to your class about issues of racial or sexual orientation.

··· NOW PLAYING ···

The Ringer

DIRECTOR: Barry W. Blaustein

STARRING: Johnny Knoxville, Luis Avalos, Katherine Heigl, Jed Rees

YEAR: 2005

RATING: PG-13 (crude and sexual humor, language, and some drug references)

RUNNING TIME: 94 min.

CORE CONCEPTS: Recreation therapy, inclusion, diversity

The idea of faking a mental disability to win the Special Olympics may sound terribly irreverent and very much like an episode of *South Park*. However, this movie was developed with the consent and support of the Special Olympics organization. Steve Barker (Knoxville) pretends to be a Special Olympian named Jeffy so he and his uncle can make some much-needed money off a bet. The real Special Olympians soon realize that "Jeffy" is only a pretender. However, they decide to keep the secret rather than let another athlete, Jimmy, win multiple years in a row.

=== SCENES ===

This movie should be shown in its entirety because of the character development and plot line. Before showing the movie, look to see if your version is "uncut." The uncut version has more sexual innuendo but is not as explicit as many current movies.

=== FRAMING ===

Before showing the movie, have students research the Special Olympics, such as how it was founded and by whom, historical developments, international events, and what competition means to the athletes.

=== DEBRIEFING QUESTIONS ===

This movie lends itself to a discussion on recreation therapy, inclusion, and diversity. Ask questions such as the following:

* How did the movie portray the Special Olympics and the Olympians? Discuss both the positive and negative aspects.
* Invite the parent or coach of a Special Olympian to discuss the movie. Ask the parent or coach whether the movie is a good depiction of the athletes and games.
* How do you think a young person with special needs might view this movie?

=== CONCEPT EXPLORATION ===

The following activities, assignments, or discussion ideas facilitate concepts from this movie:

* Go to a Special Olympics event and volunteer to be a "hugger" at the end of a race.
* The filmmakers include references to *I Am Sam* and *Forrest Gump*. How do these movies compare with *The Ringer*?
* Learn more about Special Olympics at the organization's Web site (www.specialolympics.org). Use the page to find an event in your area.

A River Runs Through It

DIRECTOR: Robert Redford

STARRING: Brad Pitt, Craig Sheffer, Tom Skerritt, Brenda Blethyn, Emily Lloyd

YEAR: 1992

RATING: PG (some brief nudity and some strong language)

RUNNING TIME: 123 min.

CORE CONCEPTS: Outdoor recreation, family issues, activity, history, diversity

The movie is narrated by Norman Maclean as an older man reflecting on his upbringing in rural Missoula, Montana. The movie takes place during the early 20th century and depicts the changes in lifestyle over a period of 40 years, including the acceptance and use of autos and telephones, the methods of courting a woman, and the importance of religious practices.

The connection between fly fishing and religion plays a major role in this movie. Brothers Norman (Craig Sheffer) and Paul (Brad Pitt) are schooled by their father in his Presbyterian manner of fly fishing. For the brothers, fishing becomes both a way to bond and a way to escape. Paul struggles with gambling and alcohol, but while he is fishing he is at his best.

Throughout the latter half of the movie, Paul's addictions lead him in a downward spiral. Norman wants to help him, but there is no way to get through except to spend time with him. At one point, Paul tells Norman that sometimes all a person needs is to know that someone wants to help.

=== SCENES ===

Because a number of core concepts come up at various times, it's best to show the movie in its entirety. Key scenes can be shown, however. The beginning of the movie, up until Norman heads off to college, depicts the boys' lives growing up in rural Montana and the importance of fly fishing as a family activity. In this part of the movie, the narrator talks briefly about how Norman worked for the Forest Service. In another scene later in the movie, Paul and Norman take their dates to a speakeasy. Paul drinks and dances with his date, a Native American, who is not welcome in the speakeasy. In one key scene, after Norman returns from Dartmouth, Paul breaks away from his father's methods of fly fishing and creates his own unique style. Norman refers to his brother as not just a fisherman but an artist, one of the highest compliments he can pay. In the final scene the father preaches about wanting to help someone who refuses the help.

═ FRAMING ═

Because this movie contains a number of core concepts, determine what you want your students to focus on. Ask questions such as the following:

* ★ What do you know about Prohibition? Was drinking a recreational pursuit during that time? Is gambling a recreational activity? Explain why some recreational activities are considered taboo.

* ★ Do you fish? Why or why not? Why is fishing such a popular recreational activity? As you watch the movie, notice the pure joy the characters in the movie experience while fishing.

* ★ What activities did you participate in with siblings or parents as a young child and teenager? What activities did you participate in with friends as a young child and teenager? How did participation in these activities shape who you are today? For instance, if you went camping with your family on a regular basis, will you continue to camp as an adult? Do you find it a way to refresh and invigorate yourself during stressful times?

═ DEBRIEFING QUESTIONS ═

The movie lends itself to a discussion on outdoor recreation, fishing, family, and diversity. Ask questions such as the following:

* ★ In what way does the Maclean family's love of fishing relate to some leisure or recreation theories? What is it about fly fishing that the boys loved so much?

* ★ What were attitudes toward Native Americans in the early 20th century, as represented in the movie? How are those attitudes mirrored in the attitudes toward other races and religions throughout history?

CONCEPT EXPLORATION

The following activities, assignments, or discussion ideas facilitate concepts from this movie:

* ★ Bring in a representative from a local outfitter who can teach fly fishing. Give each student the chance to feel the sensation of casting with a fly rod. Discuss fishing as a recreational activity. Ask students to reflect on its popularity.

* ★ Ask students to narrate a tale from their youths that involves some aspect of recreation, parks, or tourism. Perhaps they have a memory of family car trips, camping trips, or game night. How did their childhood recreational activities affect their activities as a young adult?

···NOW PLAYING···

Rize

DIRECTOR: David LaChapelle

DOCUMENTARY

YEAR: 2005

RATING: PG-13 (suggestive content, drug references, language and brief nudity)

RUNNING TIME: 84 min.

CORE CONCEPTS: Activity, diversity, competition, leisure behavior

*R*ize takes us into the world of "ghetto ballet." Children and young adults in Watts, Compton, and other depressed areas of Los Angeles have been looking up to a man named Tommy the Clown, who has taught them to express themselves through hip-hop, free expression dance. Tommy the Clown's leadership and "living by example" have kept many young people from turning to gangs and assist younger members of the community through positive mentorship. Some of Tommy's prodigies went on to develop a form of dance called Krumping, described in the movie as "battle dancing with make-up." One segment of the movie shows interconnected footage of Krumpers in Los Angeles and tribal warriors in Africa. The African footage highlights the origins of Krumping.

=== SCENES ===

This movie is best viewed in its entirety. If time is short, show as much of the movie from the beginning as time allows.

=== FRAMING ===

The best way to prepare students for this movie is to ask if they know what Krumping is or if they have ever heard of Tommy the Clown. Because this movie lends itself to four core concepts, the rest of the framing will depend on what you want the students to focus on. One way this movie can be utilized is as an introduction to activity as escape. The dancers in the movie participate as a way to focus on the positive and avoid negative, potentially dangerous paths.

=== DEBRIEFING QUESTIONS ===

This movie will leave the viewers with a fairly intense feeling. They should have a good understanding of how important dance is to the young people in the movie. Begin with a fairly general question such as "What are your immediate thoughts about the movie?" Use the responses from the students to direct further small-group discussion. Here are some possible discussion prompts:

* The Krumpers talked about using their anger to channel their dance. Do you think the clown dancers were channeling their anger as well?

* What were some of the similarities and differences between the various clown groups and the Krumpers?

* The movie received a PG-13 rating for suggestive content, drug references, language, and brief nudity. Did any of those elements stand out to you? In what way? (Chances are that your students will see all the elements as integral to the movie.)

* One young adult in the movie addressed some adults' concerns about the appropriateness of very young children dancing in what may be considered a suggestive manner. What is your opinion and why?

CONCEPT EXPLORATION

There are several ways to take discussions on *Rize* deeper and out of the classroom.

* Encourage your students to visit Tommy the Clown's Web site at www.tommytheclown.com.
* Explore the Brazilian martial art of Capoeira, either through research or observation. Capoeira was developed as a way for African slaves to fight without getting caught. They developed fight moves into a form of dance.
* Your school or community may have an active group of Krumpers.
* Compare another form of African-based dance, Stepping, to the dance in *Rize*. A movie that features Stepping is *Stomp The Yard* (2007).

· · · NOW PLAYING · · ·

Roger & Me

DIRECTOR: Michael Moore

DOCUMENTARY

YEAR: 1989

RATING: R (language)

RUNNING TIME: 91 min.

CORE CONCEPTS: Commercial recreation, tourism and travel

Michael Moore created this documentary to address the economic decline that was destroying his hometown of Flint, Michigan. General Motors chairman Roger Smith is the object of Moore's ire, although he targets others as well.

SCENES

There is really no need to show this entire movie. The most appropriate scene on the DVD is scene 24, titled "Tourist Mecca." Downtown redevelopment was initiated in Flint with the idea of luring tourists and their dollars to the area. A hotel and two attractions (including Auto World) were opened with high hopes; however, they all closed soon after opening because of a lack of visitors. The scene includes some very interesting interviews with politicians and a tourism professional speaking about the downtown redevelopment projects.

FRAMING

Give the students a worksheet with a description of Flint, Michigan, including the history of car manufacturing, population statistics, and so on. Ask them to create ideas for tourism development in the area. Use scene 24 to emphasize that sound planning must be a precursor to any tourism development.

DEBRIEFING QUESTIONS

This movie lends itself to a discussion on commercial recreation and tourism. Remind students that the focus is on sound planning. Ask questions such as the following:

* What went wrong with the Flint economic development plans? Why do you think tourists did not come?
* Was there anything Flint could have done to be successful as a tourism destination?

CONCEPT EXPLORATION

The following activities, assignments, or discussion ideas facilitate concepts from this movie:

* Have students research the current demographics, economic status, and crime rate of Flint, Michigan. Have there been any improvements since this documentary was made?

The Rookie

DIRECTOR: John Lee Hancock

STARRING: Dennis Quaid, Rachel Griffiths, Jay Hernandez, Beth Grant, Angus T. Jones, Brian Cox

YEAR: 2002

RATING: G

RUNNING TIME: 127 min.

CORE CONCEPTS: Sport, activity, teamwork, diversity, coaching

This movie is based on the true story of Jim Morris (Dennis Quaid), a father, high school teacher, and baseball coach who thought his dreams of playing professional baseball were over. To inspire his high school team, he tells them to dream and to go for the championship. They say that if they do, he will also have to follow his dreams. The team wins, and Morris goes to tryouts. He is recruited for a minor league team. After less than a season he is recruited by a major league team. This movie is about following dreams, believing in yourself and others, and relationships.

═ SCENES ═

This movie can be shown in its entirety. If time is limited, several scenes capture the essence of the movie. In the first, Jim Morris is packing up after his team's practice, and one of the players asks him if he wants to pitch a few balls. Morris throws weakly at first and then harder. He says he forgot how good the ball sounds when it lands. His son is watching him pitch. In another scene Jim goes to the tryouts and admits that he is there to try out himself, not just as a coach of his high school team. Later in the movie, Jim is partway through his season in the minor leagues and he questions whether he is doing the right thing. His wife is supportive and asks him if he still loves what he is doing. In another scene Jim enters the major league stadium for the first time as a player. His family and the entire town have come to the game to support him.

FRAMING

Provide readings on baseball or coaching. Ask questions such as the following:

★ What age is too old for players in Major League Baseball?
★ How do coaches influence their teams?

DEBRIEFING QUESTIONS

This movie lends itself to a discussion on baseball, teamwork, diversity, and coaching. Ask questions such as the following:

★ What issues related to age did Jim face as he accomplished his dreams?
★ How did the town, team, and his family support Jim?
★ What did Jim do as a coach that influenced his team?

CONCEPT EXPLORATION

The following activities, assignments, or discussion ideas facilitate concepts from this movie:

★ Research age as a factor in playing professional sports. How does age affect different sports?
★ How does coaching influence a team? Compare coaching styles.

···NOW PLAYING···

Saint Ralph

DIRECTOR: Michael McGowan

STARRING: Campbell Scott, Adam Butcher, Jennifer Tilly, Gordon Pinsent

YEAR: 2004

RATING: PG-13 (some sexual content and partial nudity)

RUNNING TIME: 98 min.

CORE CONCEPTS: Activity, competition, coaching

This movie is set in Canada in 1953 and 1954. Fourteen-year-old Ralph Walker (Adam Butcher) is in a Catholic school for boys. His father is dead, and his mother is in the hospital. He gets himself into all kinds of trouble, and the headmaster makes him join the track team. His mother goes into a coma, and he is told that it will take a miracle for her to recover. After investing a great deal of time and energy into learning about miracles, he decides to create a miracle of his own by winning the Boston Marathon.

SCENES

This movie can be shown in its entirety, but keep in mind the PG-13 rating for sexual content and language. If time is limited, several scenes show Ralph training with the cross country team. These scenes also depict the coaching that Ralph received. There are also scenes of him running and training both indoors and outdoors.

FRAMING

Provide readings on training for marathons, the history of the Boston Marathon, or coaching styles. Ask questions such as the following:

* What does it take to compete and then run in a marathon?
* What challenges do people face as they compete in long-distance endurance races?

DEBRIEFING QUESTIONS

This movie lends itself to a discussion on competition, coaching, and training for an endurance sport. Ask questions such as the following:

* How did believing in a miracle affect Ralph?
* How did Ralph's coach change his training style?

CONCEPT EXPLORATION

The following activities, assignments, or discussion ideas facilitate concepts from this movie:

* Research the history of the Boston Marathon. How did it become so famous? Who are the oldest and youngest runners to win this race?
* Research information on training for a marathon. Interview several people who are currently training or have trained for a marathon.

The Sandlot

DIRECTOR: David Mickey Evans

STARRING: Tom Guiry, Karen Allen, Denis Leary, James Earl Jones

YEAR: 1993

RATING: PG (strong language and children chewing tobacco)

RUNNING TIME: 101 min.

CORE CONCEPTS: History, life stages

This movie is set in the early 1960s and depicts the leisure activities and interests of a group of boys enjoying their summer vacation. Scotty Smalls has just moved to a new town and struggles with meeting other kids at the onset of summer. He meets up with a group of boys whose primary interest is playing baseball at a sandlot in their neighborhood. Smalls has never learned to play, even though his stepfather is a baseball fan. The boys don't take to Smalls until he makes his first catch. Once the ball falls into his glove, Smalls shows jubilation and receives instant acceptance from the others. The boys' nemesis is a huge dog that lives on the other side of the sandlot fence. The boys lose a special ball to the dog and attempt to get it back. They eventually meet the dog's owner, an ex-baseball player who is now blind. The lessons from the sandlot are many—for the boys and for your students.

SCENES

The movie is best shown in its entirety. Especially poignant scenes are those in which Smalls makes his first catch, the boys have a campout in the treehouse, and the boys visit the community pool.

FRAMING

Because there are a variety of ways to utilize this movie, make sure the students know what you want them to pay attention to. Provide readings or other materials and then ask some of these questions:

⭐ Ask students how they spent their summers as children. Did they spend more time indoors or outdoors?

* Set the stage by talking about the early days of baseball. Who were the greats? Talk about the Negro League and the politics that went along with the game.

DEBRIEFING QUESTIONS

This movie lends itself to a discussion on camaraderie between children. Give students the following questions in advance so that they can consider them as they watch the movie.

* How do the activities of the boys in the movie relate to the activities of youth today?
* How do today's youth meet playmates? Where do they spend summer days?
* What roles do recreation and sport play in today's society as compared to the early 1960s?

CONCEPT EXPLORATION

The following activities, assignments, or discussion ideas facilitate concepts from this movie:

* Consider showing this movie in conjunction with *A League of Their Own*. Both movies show eras in the history of baseball. How and why has baseball become so ingrained in American culture?
* Take your students to a local ball field for a game of baseball, softball, or kickball. Before playing, lead a discussion concerning today's extensive use of organized youth leagues in place of sandlot play. Do your students remember ever playing neighborhood pickup games?

Save the Last Dance

DIRECTOR: Thomas Carter

STARRING: Julia Stiles, Sean Patrick Thomas, Terry Kinney, Fredro Starr, Kerry Washington

YEAR: 2001

RATING: PG-13 (violence, sexual content, language, and brief drug references)

RUNNING TIME: 112 min.

CORE CONCEPTS: Leisure behavior, diversity

Sara Johnson (Julia Stiles) dreams of becoming a ballerina until her mother dies suddenly. She moves to Chicago to live with her estranged dad (Terry Kinney) and attends a new high school as one of the few white students. She becomes friends with Chenille (Kerry Washington) and eventually starts dating Chenille's brother Derek (Sean Patrick Thomas), who teaches her hip-hop dancing and encourages her to follow her dreams. The movie shows various types of dancing and how culture influences dance.

SCENES

The movie can be shown in its entirety. A good scene is the one in which Derek teaches Sara how to dance hip-hop. Several scenes illustrate racial issues of a white girl dating a black boy, as well as the stereotypes of living in certain areas of a city.

FRAMING

Provide reading on leisure, race, and ethnicity. Ask questions such as the following:

* What racial issues have you faced in leisure and recreation settings?

* How would you react if you went from being in the majority to being a minority? Has this ever happened to you? If so, what was it like?

DEBRIEFING QUESTIONS

This movie lends itself to a discussion of leisure in relation to race and ethnicity. Ask questions such as the following:

* How did peers influence the relationship between Derek and Sara?
* How did their races affect their relationship?
* How did dancing, as a form of leisure, bridge the gaps in their relationship?

CONCEPT EXPLORATION

The following activities, assignments, or discussion ideas facilitate concepts from this movie:

* Interview people who are in interracial relationships. Ask them whether recreation and leisure brought them together or kept them apart. What recreational activities do they participate in together?
* Learn a new skill that you associate with another culture or race. Spend several weeks learning the skill and keep a learning journal on the experience.

· · NOW PLAYING · · ·

Seabiscuit

DIRECTOR: Gary Ross

STARRING: Tobey Maguire, Jeff Bridges, Chris Cooper, Gary Stevens, Chris McCarrron

YEAR: 2003

RATING: PG-13 (some sexual situations and violent sports-related images)

RUNNING TIME: 141 min.

CORE CONCEPTS: Competition, sport, history, teamwork

In this movie three men come together to form a bond and train a horse that gives hope to the nation in a time of crisis. Charles Howard (Jeff Bridges) lost everything in the stock market crash of 1929, and his son was killed in an automobile accident. Tom Smith (Chris Cooper) is a cowboy without land to ride on, and Red Pollard's (Tobey Maguire) parents gave him up when the crash hit. All three men are down on their luck and are brought together to train, ride, and work with Seabiscuit, a horse who is also down on his luck. They create a racing horse that gives hope and inspiration to a nation.

═ SCENES ═

The movie can be shown in its entirety. Several scenes depict what is going on during that era in history. A few scenes right before a big race show the infield filling up with people who want Seabiscuit to win.

═ FRAMING ═

Provide some readings on the early 1900s or horse racing. Following are some suggested questions:

* How did this era affect people's recreational activities?
* In what way is a horse race recreational?

═ DEBRIEFING QUESTIONS ═

This movie lends itself to a discussion of horse racing, historical events, or spectator recreation. Questions can include the following:

* How did a horse affect a nation going through the Depression?
* In what ways did this group of men come together to become a family?

═ CONCEPT EXPLORATION ═

The following activities, assignments, or discussion ideas facilitate concepts from this movie:

* Read information about the Depression and compare what you read to the movie.
* Interview people who grew up during the Depression. Ask them about their recreational and leisure interests during that period.

★ Tour a horse racing facility and learn about how it operates, who attends the races, and how money is made by spectators, horse owners, and the facility in this sort of recreation.

Searching for Bobby Fischer

DIRECTOR: Steven Zaillian

STARRING: Joe Mantegna, Laurence Fishburne, Joan Allen, Max Pomeranc, Ben Kingsley

YEAR: 1993

RATING: PG (thematic elements)

RUNNING TIME: 110 min.

CORE CONCEPTS: Competition, sport, family issues, coaching, leisure behavior

Josh Waitzkin (Max Pomeranc) is a seven-year-old who has a gift for chess. He is also a typical seven-year-old who plays sports, fishes with his dad, and has friends. He is fascinated by chess, and his father gets him a tutor. He ends up winning many tournaments, and his father is supportive and loves that he is winning. The game of chess becomes more than a game for Josh, who starts to feel scared about how his father will react if he loses. He purposely loses and is told he does not have to play anymore. Josh decides to continue to play for himself and for the love of playing.

═══ SCENES ═══

This movie can be shown in its entirety, or several scenes can be shown. In one scene Josh is playing chess with his dad. Josh keeps losing, so his mom and dad give him permission to win. He plays his dad again, and while his dad struggles over each move, Josh talks on the phone, takes a bath, and does other things; he still beats his father. In another scene Josh's father observes a chess tournament and talks to Josh's soon-to-be coach about how some see chess as a game, but to others it is an art. Later in the film, at the first tournament that Josh plays in, the tournament director asks the parents not to be involved and not to coach their children. The parents keep interfering and are taken into the basement to wait for their children to finish. In another scene Josh and his father talk about not going to the state competition. Josh explains that one of the reasons he does not want to play is that being the top-ranked chess player invites a lot of pressure. Josh is also referring to the pressure his dad puts on him.

FRAMING

Provide some readings on coaching or parental pressure in youth sports. Ask questions such as the following:

* What challenges do recreation programmers face in regard to parental pressure on youth in recreational activities?
* Have you seen parental pressure affect youth in sports and competition? What did it look like?
* How does competition affect youth at early ages?

DEBRIEFING QUESTIONS

This movie lends itself to a discussion on competition, youth activities, parental pressure, coaching, or being well rounded as a competitor. Debriefing questions may include the following:

* What style of coaching did you see during the movie, and who did the coaching?
* What pressures did Josh face as a young competitor?
* What other activities do some view as a game and others view as an art?

CONCEPT EXPLORATION

The following activities, assignments, or discussion ideas facilitate concepts from this movie:

* Research and write a report on several young people who have achieved great things in their sport or activity. What did they go through to get there? How did their families support them? Who coached them, and how did this work?
* Compare the various coaching styles in this movie to coaching styles in other movies.
* Attend a chess tournament and observe the players. What do you notice about them?

Shall We Dance?

DIRECTOR: Peter Chelsom

STARRING: Richard Gere, Jennifer Lopez, Susan Sarandon, Lisa Ann Walter, Stanley Tucci

YEAR: 2004

RATING: PG-13 (some sexual references and brief language)

RUNNING TIME: 106 min.

CORE CONCEPTS: Competition, leisure behavior, coaching

John Clark (Richard Gere) is an overworked family man who writes wills for a living. Through curiosity and a desire to meet Paulina (Jennifer Lopez), he enrolls in dance lessons. He is very uncoordinated at first but eventually learns to dance and develops a friendship with Paulina and a love for dancing. He keeps this a secret from his family as he trains for a big dance competition. His love for dancing eventually transfers into his life.

═ SCENES ═

This movie can be shown in its entirety. If time is limited, several scenes can be shown. In one scene John goes into the dance studio and enrolls in classes. He is looking around and trying to figure out if he fits in. In another scene he is on the subway thinking about how his clients change sometimes after they have visited him, and he reflects on the influence he sometimes has on his clients. You might also show the scene at the dance competition when John is dancing and sees his wife and daughter watching him.

═ FRAMING ═

Provide readings on dance lessons, the history of dance, or dance competitions. Ask questions such as the following:

★ What leisure activities do you participate in that make you happy?

★ At what stage in people's lives do they change leisure pursuits?

★ How can people involve their families in their leisure interests?

DEBRIEFING QUESTIONS

This movie lends itself to a discussion on dance, competition, leisure behavior, and passion. Ask questions such as the following:

* What struggles and challenges did John face as he learned to dance?
* Why did dancing make him happy?
* How did family and friends support John in his interests?
* In what way was Paulina John's dancing coach?

CONCEPT EXPLORATION

The following activities, assignments, or discussion ideas facilitate concepts from this movie:

* Try a new skill that you did not think you would be able to do, such as dancing. Keep a journal on how you feel during the learning process. Interview others who are also learning a new skill.
* Go to a dance competition or another leisure activity competition that you have not seen before. What do you notice? Ask competitors why they participate. What parts of the competition do they enjoy, and what parts do they not enjoy?
* Compare this movie to other movies about dance or dance competitions. What similarities and differences do you see?

· · · NOW PLAYING · · ·

A Shot at Glory

DIRECTOR: Michael Corrente

STARRING: Robert Duvall, Michael Keaton, Ally McCoist, Brian Cox, Cole Hauser, Kirsty Mitchell

YEAR: 2000

RATING: R (language and brief sexuality)

RUNNING TIME: 114 min.

CORE CONCEPTS: Sport, coaching, teamwork, history

This movie is about a Scottish second-tier football team managed by Gordon McLeod (Robert Duvall). The American owner of the team (Michael Keaton) is pressuring the team to win. Gordon must face his own demons as he manages the team to play against the Rangers.

SCENES

This movie can be shown in its entirety to illustrate teamwork, coaching, and a view of football in Scotland. If time is an issue, show the first three minutes, during which the narrator talks about the history of football in Scotland between two Scottish teams, the Celtics and the Rangers.

FRAMING

Briefly explain to a U.S. audience that "soccer" is known as "football" throughout most of the world. Provide readings on Scotland and the history of football. Ask questions such as the following:

* What does true rivalry look like?
* When have you experienced rivalry?

DEBRIEFING QUESTIONS

This movie lends itself to a discussion on sports, coaching, and teamwork. A comparison can be made between football in Scotland and football in the United States. Ask questions such as the following:

* How do the fans and money influence this team?
* What influence does the United States have on football in Scotland?
* What coaching style was used in this movie?

CONCEPT EXPLORATION

The following activities, assignments, or discussion ideas facilitate concepts from this movie:

* Research the history of football in Scotland. How has it changed over time? In what way is the United States currently involved with football in other countries?
* Compare this movie to other movies about competition, sports, or coaching.

Steel Magnolias

DIRECTOR: Herbert Ross

STARRING: Sally Field, Dolly Parton, Shirley MacLaine, Daryl Hannah, Olympia Dukakis, Julia Roberts, Tom Skerrit, Sam Shepard, Dylan McDermott

YEAR: 1989

RATING: PG (brief nudity, adult situations, and language)

RUNNING TIME: 117 min.

CORE CONCEPTS: Health and wellness, leisure behavior, family issues

This movie is set in the 1980s in Louisiana and tells the story of a group of friends whose lives come together around a beauty parlor. The movie depicts their lives, their celebrations and tragedies, and their support for each other. Shelby (Julia Roberts) has diabetes, and much of the movie revolves around her relationship to her mother as she gets married and has a child.

SCENES

This movie can be shown in its entirety. If time is limited, show two scenes set in the beauty shop. In one scene Shelby is getting her hair done for the wedding and has a diabetic seizure. This scene shows how the others react and what a diabetic seizure looks like. In another scene Shelby wants to cut her hair off, which illustrates that she is starting over and needs something new.

FRAMING

Provide readings on diabetics and how diabetes affects people's lives. Ask questions such as the following:

* Have you ever known someone with diabetes? If so, how did it affect that person's life and specifically their recreational interests?

* As someone who may work with a person with diabetes in the future, what information do you need to know?

DEBRIEFING QUESTIONS

This movie lends itself to a discussion on family and friendship, health and wellness, and leisure behavior. Ask questions such as the following:

* How did these women support each other?
* What role did recreation play in their lives?
* How did the relationship between Shelby and her mother influence her recreation choices and her life?
* How does diabetes affect Shelby and her life and recreation choices?

CONCEPT EXPLORATION

The following activities, assignments, or discussion ideas facilitate concepts from this movie:

* Research diabetes and other diseases that affect people on a daily basis. What can you do as a recreation professional to assist people with such diseases in your future programs?
* Interview people with diabetes. How does it affect their recreational and leisure interests? Are they restricted in what they can do? What do recreation leaders need to learn to help people with diabetes?

· · · NOW PLAYING · · ·

Super Size Me

DIRECTOR: Morgan Spurlock

DOCUMENTARY

YEAR: 2004

RATING: PG (thematic elements, a disturbing medical procedure, and some language)

RUNNING TIME: 100 min.

CORE CONCEPTS: Leisure behavior, health and wellness

ocumentarian Morgan Spurlock explores the fast-food industry in the United States. He spends 30 days on a "McDiet," eating only McDonald's food. While his body undergoes some surprising changes, he investigates the power of the fast-food industry and the effect it has on the U.S. population. Spurlock focuses heavily on the marketing efforts of the food industry and how young children are lured into the "McHabit" of eating fast food.

Spurlock's physical changes are monitored by three physicians and a nutritionist. Some medical scenes are graphic, and there is a candid discussion of the sexual side effects of the 30-day McDonald's binge. *Super Size Me* leaves a lasting impression of the realities of American eating habits, the health impact of obesity, and the fact that fast food is embedded in our culture.

SCENES

The movie can be shown in its entirety. If time is an issue, show the scene in which Spurlock visits a school lunchroom. He interviews children, teachers, and administrators in an attempt to understand nutritional awareness. Another excellent scene is the one in which Spurlock shows young children a series of photos of "prominent" people. This is an excellent starting point for a discussion of the impact of the food industry's marketing efforts.

FRAMING

Provide some reading on leisure and healthy lives. Ask questions such as the following:

* What is healthy leisure?
* Are eating and dining out considered leisure activities? How do they affect leisure?
* How often do you eat out? Have often do you eat fast food?

DEBRIEFING QUESTIONS

In this movie Spurlock interviews people on the street and children in a school. Pose his questions to your students. Debriefing questions can also include the following:

* How does eating affect someone's leisure? Health? Social situations?
* Do you think people from different age groups would view the movie differently?

* What are your earliest memories of fast food?
* How has fast food become part of popular culture?

═══ CONCEPT EXPLORATION ═══

The following activities, assignments, or discussion ideas facilitate concepts from this movie:

* An "educationally enhanced" DVD of *Super Size Me* is available and includes curriculum lessons for middle school and high school students.

* *Super Size Me* can be shown in conjunction with *Fast Food Nation,* a 2006 movie based on the *New York Times* bestselling book *Fast Food Nation* by Eric Schlosser. Assigning readings from the book, such as the chapter "Why the Fries Taste Good," would be an excellent way to augment students' understanding of fast food in America.

Following are additional activities:

* Keep a personal food journal for one week, monitoring what you eat and where you eat. Make notes on how you feel before you eat and after you eat. Do you eat alone or in a social setting? Were you hungry before you ate? Try to measure your caloric intake at each meal.

* Count the number of McDonald's (or other fast-food) restaurants in your community. Compare that number to the area's population. Calculate the number of restaurants per square mile.

* Observe diners in a fast-food restaurant. How many are children? How long do people stay? How many cars go through the drive-thru in a given period of time?

* If you are studying facility management, assess the play structures at restaurants. Do they comply with playground safety standards?

Take the Lead

DIRECTOR: Liz Friedlander

STARRING: Antonio Banderas, Rob Brown, Alfre Woodard, Dante Basco, Ray Liotta, Lyriq Bent

YEAR: 2006

RATING: PG-13 (thematic material, language, and some violence)

RUNNING TIME: 108 min.

CORE CONCEPTS: Leadership, coaching, teamwork, activity

This movie is based on the true story of ballroom dancer Pierre Dulaine (Antonio Banderas), who volunteered to teach ballroom dancing in the New York public school system. He is assigned to the students who are in detention, and conflicts soon arise over tastes in music. The movie shows how their relationship develops. The students eventually compete in a dance competition.

═ SCENES ═

This movie can be shown in its entirety; if time is limited, two scenes can be shown. In the first, the school principal is telling the other teachers about Pierre Dulaine. She explains that learning ballroom dancing will be a form of punishment for the students. In another scene Dulaine has to defend the dancing at a parent–teacher conference. He demonstrates by dancing with the principal and explains that dancing teaches respect and dignity.

═ FRAMING ═

Provide readings on leisure education, leisure and recreation in public schools, or competition. Ask questions such as the following:

- ★ What sort of leisure education did you have in high school?
- ★ What form of leisure education is currently being provided in public schools?
- ★ What is the value of leisure education in public schools?
- ★ How does dancing influence people? What life skills does it teach?

DEBRIEFING QUESTIONS

This movie lends itself to a discussion on leadership, teamwork, and dance. Ask questions such as the following:

* What is the value of competition and dancing for these students?
* What other areas of their lives might social dance influence?
* How can one person make a difference in the lives of others through recreation and sport?

CONCEPT EXPLORATION

The following activities, assignments, or discussion ideas facilitate concepts from this movie:

* Visit local public schools and learn about the types of leisure education they provide. Interview students, principals, teachers, and parents.
* Research social dance (either by taking a social dance class or by interviewing people who dance on a regular basis). What do people gain from social dance experiences?

· · · NOW PLAYING · · ·

Touching the Void

DIRECTOR: Kevin Macdonald

STARRING: Joe Simpson, Simon Yates, Richard Hawking, Nicholas Aaron, Brendan Mackey

YEAR: 2003

RATING: R (language)

RUNNING TIME: 106 min.

CORE CONCEPTS: Outdoor recreation, leadership, teamwork, physical and mental challenge

This movie tells the true story of two British friends, Joe Simpson and Simon Yates, who conquered the unclimbed west face of 21,000-foot peak Siula Grande in Peru in 1985. Decision making, leadership, and teamwork are challenged as Joe and Simon descend the mountain. Joe, Simon, and Richard Hawking—their campsite guard—narrate their story as actors (Nicholas Aaron and Brendan Mackey) depict the action.

SCENES

This movie can be shown in its entirety. Specific scenes are challenging to find. In a scene that illustrates decision making, Joe is in a crevasse and has to decide what to do. He states the importance of making a decision in a wilderness situation, especially a tragic one such as his.

FRAMING

Provide some readings on wilderness expeditions, decision making, leadership, or goal setting. Ask questions such as the following:

* Have you ever been in a situation in which you had to make a decision and later had to reflect on and evaluate that decision?
* Have you ever set a small goal for yourself? Have you ever faced a big obstacle? How do the two situations compare?

DEBRIEFING QUESTIONS

This movie lends itself to a discussion on decision making, leadership, and teamwork. Ask questions such as the following:

* Where did you see teamwork in this movie?
* How did decision making affect the lives of these three men in the wilderness?
* How does the wilderness expedition depicted in this movie compare to other wilderness expeditions you are familiar with?

CONCEPT EXPLORATION

The following activities, assignments, or discussion ideas facilitate concepts from this movie:

* Research several wilderness expeditions. What roles do group dynamics, leadership, and decision making play in the wilderness context?
* Interview people who do extreme activities. What motivates them to participate in these activities?

Trekkies

DIRECTOR: Roger Nygard

DOCUMENTARY

YEAR: 1997

RATING: PG (for mild sexual and drug references)

RUNNING TIME: 87 min.

CORE CONCEPTS: Leisure behavior, commercial recreation, tourism and travel

The original *Star Trek* series aired on television from 1966 to 1969. The fervor of the fans only grew in the years after the series went into reruns. A number of television series and movies aired in the decades following the original. The die-hard fans—Trekkies or Trekkers, depending on whom you are speaking with—live and breathe the *Star Trek* mythology. They spend millions on memorabilia and travel to attend theme conventions. The movie, *Trekkies*, introduces the viewer to the people who are active participants in the *Star Trek* phenomenon. Trekkies are interviewed at conventions, at home, and at their places of business. The viewer is able to see how deeply a hobby can become a way of life. One of the most enlightening aspects of this documentary is that people from all age groups, professions, and income brackets participate.

═ SCENES ═

Trekkies can be viewed in its entirety; however, it's possible students may feel that they "get the point" early on and tune out. If you prefer to show only part of the movie, select a series of scenes.

Scene 1 ("Opening Sequence") is important because it sets up the concept of a Trekkie. Scene 4 introduces the viewer to Barbara Adams, a fan who sat on a rather important jury in full *Star Trek* uniform. In scene 19, we follow Barbara to her place of business, where she prefers to be referred to as "The Commander." Scene 5 ("The First Convention") shows stars from the original *Star Trek* television series talking about the first fan conventions. Scene 8 ("Fan or Fanatic") explores the difference between a fan and a fanatic. Scene 12 ("Changing Lives") includes interviews of stars from various *Star Trek* series telling stories about their involvement with fans. Scenes 24 and 25 are related to the topic of tourism. Scene 24 ("James T. Kirk") ends with the relevance of a small Iowa town to *Star Trek*. Scene 25 ("Welcome to Vulcan") begins with the relevance of a small town in Canada.

FRAMING

Since many young people are not overly familiar with *Star Trek*, consider showing a classic *Star Trek* episode (such as "The Trouble With Tribbles") to get them familiar with the characters. Develop a worksheet for students to complete regarding their most passionate leisure pursuits.

★ What are you "really into"?

★ Are you a fan of any sport, television show, or music group?

★ Would you consider yourself to be fanatical about anything?

DEBRIEFING QUESTIONS

Try not to let viewers walk away from the movie thinking that *Star Trek* fans are crazy. Get students thinking about how fanaticism is displayed in other areas of life.

★ *Star Trek* fans are "really into it." Can you think of other fans who are really "into" something? Compare Trekkies to Foodies (fans of food), oenophiles (wine lovers), or some other more mainstream group of people.

★ Compare NASCAR fans to Trekkies.

★ Someone in the movie refers to Barbara Adams as "brave." What is the difference, in this case, between brave and obsessed?

As an interesting aside: Gabriel Köerner, the youngest fan profiled in the movie, has gone on to be a successful digital artist. Check out his filmography by searching for his name on www.imdb.com.

Be sure to end class by saying "Live long and prosper!"

CONCEPT EXPLORATION

There are a number of ways to get students involved with the serious leisure of fans. (See the *Project Grizzly* entry for more information about serious leisure.)

* If there is a fan convention anywhere near your town, take your students. Have them informally interview attendees about their interests. Consider asking some of the same questions that were addressed in the movie.

* If no convention is available, look for midnight showings of movies such as *The Rocky Horror Picture Show* or *The Adventures of Priscilla, Queen of the Desert*. Both movies have fans who dress up and "become" a character for the movie showings. What makes these people so consumed by a movie?

* Perhaps you are more readily able to access a large group of sports fans. Are the fans who paint their bodies, wear team gear from head to toe, and recite player statistics on par with *Star Trek* fans?

* The interesting tourism and travel connection of this movie is set up in scenes 24 and 25. Riverside, Iowa, wanted to increase its economic development through tourism. They decided to capitalize on being mentioned in an episode of *Star Trek* as the town where Captain Kirk was born on March 22, 2228! Riverside now hosts the annual Trek Fest (www.trekfest.com) and was featured on a reality television special in which William Shatner (who played the character of Kirk) conned the town into thinking he was filming a movie there.

We Are Marshall

DIRECTOR: McG

STARRING: Matthew McConaughey, Matthew Fox, Anthony Mackie, Davis Strathairn, Ian McShane

YEAR: 2006

RATING: PG (emotional thematic material, a crash scene, and mild language)

RUNNING TIME: 124 min.

CORE CONCEPTS: Teamwork, coaching

This movie is based on the true story of a 1970 plane crash that killed almost the entire varsity football team of Marshall University. With the help of head coach Jack Lengyel (Matthew McConaughey), the football team slowly develops again and hope is given to the community. Red Dawson (Matthew Fox), the assistant coach who was not on the plane when it crashed, eventually helps Jack build a new football team.

SCENES

The movie can be shown in its entirety. If time is limited, several scenes capture the theme of the movie. In one scene the president of the university visits Jack Lengyel to find out why he wants to coach the football team. Lengyel states that he wants to help. In another scene Lengyel is talking to Red to convince him to come back to the team. They discuss the difference between playing to win and playing for the love of the game. Later in the movie the coach takes the team to the gravesites of six of the players who died in the plane crash. This helps motivate the team to come together and play from their hearts.

FRAMING

Provide readings on the history of collegiate sports, the rules and regulations of the NCAA (Marshall was able to get an exception to these rules), or coaching styles. Ask questions such as the following:

* What struggles do you think you would face if you coached a team that had experienced a great tragedy?
* How can coaching a team influence a community?

DEBRIEFING QUESTIONS

Discussion topics can include issues related to coaching, teamwork, tragedy, or sports. Ask questions such as the following:

* What did you like about Jack Lengyel's coaching style?
* What challenges did the team face in its efforts to rebuild itself?
* How does a community affect a sport team?

CONCEPT EXPLORATION

The following activities, assignments, or discussion ideas facilitate concepts from this movie:

* Read about Marshall University and the history that inspired this movie. What parts of history were not included? How did this influence the movie?
* Compare this movie on coaching with other movies about sports and coaching. What similarities do you see in coaching styles? What challenges did the various coaches face, and how did they face those challenges? In your opinion, what are the characteristics of an ideal coach?

··· NOW PLAYING ···

The Young and the Dead

DIRECTORS: Robert Pulcini, Shari Springer Berman

DOCUMENTARY

YEAR: 2000

RATING: NR (not rated)

RUNNING TIME: 91 min.

CORE CONCEPT: Commercial recreation

This film is a documentary of the revival of the Hollywood Memorial Cemetery in Los Angeles, California. Reopened by Tyler Cassity and renamed Hollywood Forever, the cemetery memorializes people through 15-minute movies documenting their lives.

Cassity runs Hollywood Forever with the assistance of friends and family. The camaraderie of the group is evident. Cassity has a wonderful understanding of leisure and recreation spaces. Highlights of the film include interviews with regular visitors to the cemetery, a wedding at the facility, and a Halloween fundraiser.

SCENES

This movie is best shown in its entirety.

FRAMING

Explain that some parks and recreation departments are responsible for communities' cemeteries. Ask questions such as the following:

* Have you ever spent leisure time in a cemetery?
* Do you think cemeteries are acceptable recreation areas?

DEBRIEFING QUESTIONS

This movie lends itself to a discussion on leisure recreation. To facilitate group discussion, ask questions such as the following:

* What was your initial reaction to this movie?
* Do you think Cassity and his coworkers are brilliant or crazy?
* What types of recreation activities were visitors to the cemetery participating in? What activities can attract visitors to a cemetery? (Explain that many visitors to cemeteries engage in painting, photography, bird-watching, walking for exercise, marker rubbing, and genealogy, as well as harmful or destructive recreation because of the solitude such places offer.)

CONCEPT EXPLORATION

The following activities, assignments, or discussion ideas facilitate concepts from this movie:

* Meet with your class or group at a local cemetery to pick up trash and make simple repairs.
* Take one or more friends to a cemetery to participate in a recreational activity. Document your friends' reactions. Explain to your friends that many cemeteries are important community areas.

Conclusion: That's a Wrap!

We hope you had a few "Aha!" moments as you looked through *Teaching With Movies: Recreation, Sports, Tourism, and Physical Education*. Perhaps you found an entry for your favorite movie, but you had never thought to use it as a teaching tool. Perhaps you had been struggling to find an appropriate way to frame a difficult topic, and you discovered a scene from a film that would work perfectly.

You may want to conduct further research on certain movies to help you prepare framing and debriefing activities. In the introduction to this book, we noted that we had gathered information on films from a number of resources. We found the following Web sites particularly useful:

- The Internet Movie Database (www.imdb.com)
- The Classification and Rating Administration (www.filmratings.com)
- Blockbuster (www.blockbuster.com)
- Yahoo! Movies (www.movies.yahoo.com)
- Common Sense Media (www.commonsensemedia.org)

In addition, many studios have created specific Web sites for movies as a promotional tool. Movie fans also create Web sites to encourage discussion and share their love of film. To discover Web sites for a particular movie, just type the title of the film into your favorite search engine. (Be sure to enclose the title in quotation marks to increase the chances of a productive search.)

An excellent Web site for viewing movie trailers, as well as television clips, is http://videodetective.com. You will find trailers and movie information for both current and classic films. The movies are easy to locate by title, genre, decade, rating, and actors.

If you are involved in parks and recreation education and are not a member of the online listserv SPREnet, please consider joining. A listserv is an electronic tool utilized by people who share an interest to communicate via mass e-mail. SPREnet is a listserv for members of the Society of Park and Recreation Educators (SPRE), which is a branch of the National Recreation and Park Association (NRPA). Membership on the listserv will allow you to be an active participant in online discussions about teaching methods and receive various campus and agency announcements, among other pieces of information. It's a great way to discover how others like yourself use movies, textbooks, and other resources in the classroom.

For details on how to join the listserv, (1) visit the NRPA home page at www.nrpa.org, (2) click on "About NRPA," (3) click on "Branches and Sections," and (4) follow the SPRE link to see the branch's page.

So many movies could be used to address topics in recreation, sports, tourism, and physical education that we could not include them all in one guide. Therefore, we have created an online wiki page—a collaborative Web site for discussing the use of movies as teaching tools. We invite you to visit our wiki and contribute your thoughts on the films and techniques in this book, as well as your own favorite movies and methods. To access the wiki, visit the Human Kinetics Web site at www.humankinetics.com, search for this book (by author, title, ISBN, or keyword), and follow the link.

We look forward to reading your comments and sharing creative instruction!

References

Davis, J.R. (1993). *Better teaching, more learning: Strategies for success in postsecondary settings*. Phoenix, AZ: Oryx.

Duncan, C.A., Nolan, J., & Wood, R. (2002, October). See you in the movies? We hope not! *JOPERD—The Journal of Physical Education, Recreation & Dance, 73* (8), 38-44.

Fain, T.A. (2004). American popular culture: Should we integrate it into American education? *Education, 124* (4), 590-595.

Marshall, J. (2002). *What would Buffy do? The use of popular culture examples in undergraduate library instruction*. Paper presented at the annual meeting of the Popular Culture Association and American Culture Association, Toronto, Ontario, Canada, March 13-16.

Prensky, M. (2001). Digital natives, digital immigrants. *On the Horizon, 9* (5), 1-6.

Robinson, M.B. (2000, March). Using active learning in criminal justice: Twenty-five examples [Electronic version]. *Journal of Criminal Justice Education, 11* (1), 65-78. Routledge.

Rogers, E.E. (2002). *Waiting to exhale: African American women and adult learning through movies*. Paper presented at the annual meeting of the Adult Education Research Conference, Raleigh, North Carolina, May 24-26. For full text: www.edst.educ.ubc.ca/aerc/2002/papers/Rogers.pdf.

Rushkoff, D. (1996). *Playing the future: How kids' culture can teach us to thrive in an age of chaos*. New York: HarperCollins.

Stebbins, R.A. (2000). *World Leisure International position statement on educating for serious leisure*. World Leisure Commission on Education. Retrieved March 14, 2007, from www.worldleisure.org.

Turner, G. (1999). *Film as social practice* (3rd ed.). London: Routledge.

Wilson, M.E. (2004, Summer). Teaching, learning, and millennial students [Electronic version]. *New Directions for Student Services, 106*, 59-71.

Wlodkowski, R. (1978). *Motivation and teaching: A practical guide*. Washington, DC: National Education Association.

Young, J.R. (2002, December 6). Homework? What homework? [Electronic version]. *The Chronicle of Higher Education, 49*. Retrieved June 29, 2006, from http://chronicle.com/chronicle/v49/4915guide.htm.

About the Authors

Teresa O'Bannon, PhD, is an assistant professor in the department of recreation, parks and tourism at Radford University in Radford, Virginia. An avid movie buff since seeing *Jaws* as a child, she has been teaching and working in the field of recreation, parks, and tourism for over 15 years. You can find a link to her personal Web site by looking up this book on the Human Kinetics Web site (www.HumanKinetics.com). On her Web site she hosts movie discussions by recreation teachers. In her spare time, Dr. O'Bannon likes—what else?—watching movies and television shows, reading current-event magazines, and—despite what she saw in *Jaws*—snorkeling.

Marni Goldenberg, PhD, is an assistant professor in the recreation, parks, and tourism administration program at California Polytechnic State University in San Luis Obispo. She has been teaching full time at Cal Poly since 2003. Dr. Goldenberg uses movies in her classroom as a teaching tool and frequently relates the topics of the course to popular culture movies. She received her PhD from the University of Minnesota in 2002. Dr. Goldenberg has researched and presented on the use of movies as educational tools. In her leisure time, she enjoys hiking, mountain biking, climbing, running with her dog, and being outdoors.